NETWORK EMPOWERMENT

NATO Science Series

A series presenting the results of scientific meetings supported under the NATO Science Programme.

The series is published by IOS Press and Kluwer Academic Publishers in conjunction with the NATO Scientific Affairs Division.

Sub-Series

I.	Life and Behavioural Sciences	IOS Press
II.	Mathematics, Physics and Chemistry	Kluwer Academic Publishers
III.	Computer and Systems Sciences	IOS Press
IV.	Earth and Environmental Sciences	Kluwer Academic Publishers
V.	Science and Technology Policy	IOS Press

The NATO Science Series continues the series of books published formerly as the NATO ASI Series.

The NATO Science Programme offers support for collaboration in civil science between scientists of countries of the Euro-Atlantic Partnership Council. The types of scientific meeting generally supported are "Advanced Study Institutes" and "Advanced Research Workshops", although other types of meeting are supported from time to time. The NATO Science Series collects together the results of these meetings. The meetings are co-organized by scientists from NATO countries and scientists from NATO's Partner countries – countries of the CIS and Central and Eastern Europe.

Advanced Study Institutes are high-level tutorial courses offering in-depth study of latest advances in a field.
Advanced Research Workshops are expert meetings aimed at critical assessment of a field, and identification of directions for future action.

As a consequence of the restructuring of the NATO Science Programme in 1999, the NATO Science Series has been re-organized and there are currently five sub-series as noted above. Please consult the following web sites for information on previous volumes published in the series, as well as details of earlier sub-series:

http://www.nato.int/science
http://www.wkap.nl
http://www.iospress.nl
http://www.wtv-books.de/nato_pco.htm

Series III: Computer and Systems Sciences - Vol. 192 ISSN 1387-6694

Network Empowerment

Edited by

Oliver B. Popov

Mid Sweden University, Sundsvall, Sweden

IOS Press

Amsterdam • Berlin • Oxford • Tokyo • Washington, DC

Published in cooperation with NATO Scientific Affairs Division

Proceedings of the NATO Advanced Networking Workshop on Engineering the Network
16–26 August 2001
Budapest, Hungary

ISBN 1 58603 427 8
Library of Congress Control Number: 2004105155

Publisher
IOS Press
Nieuwe Hemweg 6B
1013 BG Amsterdam
Netherlands
fax: +31 20 620 3419
e-mail: order@iospress.nl

Distributor in the UK and Ireland
IOS Press/Lavis Marketing
73 Lime Walk
Headington
Oxford OX3 7AD
England
fax: +44 1865 750079

Distributor in the USA and Canada
IOS Press, Inc.
4502 Rachael Manor Drive
Fairfax, VA 22032
USA
fax: +1 703 323 3668
e-mail: iosbooks@iospress.com

PRINTED IN THE NETHERLANDS

Contents

CEENet Workshops on Network Technology

This is the age of information and the Internet. It is based on the blend of two powerful technologies such as telecommunications and computing, which emerged in the second half of the twentieth century. Their omnipresence has a profound and lasting impression in the way people work, live and interact with each other. The ability to communicate globally creates the fabric of the information economy that is largely based on the production and distribution of information and information services.

Science and education are one of the main pillars of every contemporary society. Therefore, the importance of networking in research and higher education has been recognized by many countries with the establishment of National Research and Education Networks (NRENs). While mainly focused on the higher education and cutting-edge research, NRENs have also become springboards for many services and applications to certain sectors of the government, elementary and secondary education, civic and non-governmental organizations.

The Central and Eastern European Networking Association (CEENet), founded in 1994, comprises of the national research and education networks from 25 countries in the CEE region, and FSU countries including the Caucasus and Central Asia. Rather early, CEENet introduced the institute of workshops on technological, managerial and policy levels, as a key instrument to improve the know-how with respect to networking and the Internet technology to its members and to promote their merits and benefits across the academic communities.

The workshops have become important events where students have the opportunity to acquire engineering skills in building an efficient and flexible networking infrastructure, to identify major services and the ways how these systems are developed and managed, to design the architecture and the content of the network information systems, and finally to exploit the advantages of distance education.

CEENet has been blessed to collaborate with the exceptional individuals from the international organizations such as NATO Science Committee and Soros Foundation. Those two organizations have provided the necessary funds for making the workshops possible by displaying remarkable ability to sense the needs of many developing countries for access to variety of information sources and to assist CEENet in educating the young and the best in those countries how to build the necessary infrastructure and to develop the content to be distributed all across the network systems.

In addition, many major corporations are behind the CEENet efforts in education by providing the workshops with sophisticated equipment (both hardware and software) and lecturers. The list of companies includes Cisco Systems, Sun Microsystems, GlobCommunications, 3 Com, Oracle, HP, Newbridge Networks, Juniper Networks, and O'Reilly and Associates.

The primary objectives of the Workshops have been to train people involved in national networking projects, to expand their knowledge about computer networking, to raise the Internet awareness and to underline the importance of accessible and sometimes free information sources.

The trainees of the workshop have had the opportunity to learn about the most advanced and yet affordable networking concepts through lectures, laboratory exercises, intensive discussions, round tables and group projects. The students have the privilege to meet the leaders in academic and corporate communities also, which gives them an ample opportunity to explore venues for co-operation in the future.

The network technology workshop series includes the events in Warsaw (1995), Budapest (1996, 1999, 2000, and 2001), Zagreb (1997), and Bratislava (1998). Whenever possible, CEENet has published proceedings from the workshops, which represent selections of the most relevant topics and papers.

This book includes materials from the workshops on network technology that took place in 2000 and 2001 in Budapest. It covers a range of topics such as Quality of Service (QoS), TCP performance related to congestion management, security issues in open systems, schemes for tariffing and micro-payments so much needed in the realm of e-business, cashing mechanisms and content delivery, the ubiquity of the Internet, the experience from a unique multicountry distance education project, and finally a comparative analysis of a few well-known e-learning environments.

The articles and the Workshop behind them, time and again, document the continuous efforts of CEENet in network empowerment provided to more than six hundred people over the period of nine years. Today, they are in the forefront of Information and Communication Technology in their respective countries, bringing closer the information horizons of the Internet and the high-performance networking, firstly to the academic communities, and secondly to other segments of the society, which eventually leads to overall progress and better future for everyone.

Oliver Popov

This book is dedicated to the memory of Professor Tomasz Hofmokl, who was the first Chairman of CEENet, serving two consequitive terms from 1993 until 1997. Professor Hofmokl was a pioneer of networking and the Internet in Poland, and both the founder and the director of NASK (Research and Academic Computer Network of Poland) until his untimely death.

Network Empowerment
O.B. Popov (Ed.)
IOS Press, 2004

François Fluckiger

Improving the Quality of Service on the Internet

1. Introduction

The Internet transport technology was designed to be robust, resilient to link or node outages, and with no single point of failure. The resulting connectionless system supports what is called a "best effort datagram delivery service", the performance of which is often greatly unpredictable. To improve the predictability of IP-based networks, several Quality of Service technologies have been designed over the past decade. The first one, RSVP, based on reservation of resources, is operational but has several major deficiencies, such as scalability difficulties. However, associated to other more recent technologies - RSVP aggregation, Diffserv and MPLS - the combination may result into an appropriate solution for improving Quality of Service guarantees in a scalable way.

2. Back to basics: The Internet transport service

One of the principal reasons for the success of the Internet lies in its *transport* technology. What is so special with the Internet transport technology? Unlike all the other wide area network technologies such as the Switched Telephone Network, X.25, ATM or Frame Relay, the Internet is not connection-oriented. This means that no prior connection between the two communicating systems - we say the *"end-systems"* - is required before a first fragment of information - the *packet*, also called the *datagram* - can be sent. As a result, all packets, which are treated independently by the network, must carry the full address of the destination system.

Packets may also take differing *routes* to reach the destination, though in practice, this only happens in case of link or node failure. If they take differing routes, they may be delivered not in an orderly way, as a given packet may take over another one on the different path. More importantly, packets may be lost, for reasons we examine later. If a packet is lost, the end-systems are not informed, and they have to detect such loses by themselves -as long as it matters for them to know about data losses. What the network guarantees is that it will do *"its best"* to deliver these datagrams. This is why the resulting Internet transport service is called a *best-effort datagram delivery service*.

Each of these base techniques, *connection-less* and *connection-oriented* have their own merits and drawbacks:

- In a *connection-less* network, there is no delay needed to set up a connection between the two communicating systems, before a first data packet can be sent. This is by the way, a fundamental feature of the Internet transport technology which was key in the support of the main Internet application: The World Wide Web. Indeed, imagine if, when you click on a link, a hard connection - that is a sort of telephone call - had be set over the network before the first packet of your request be sent to the destination (well, in practice, there is a first handshake called the TCP connection, but this is very fast as it only involves the two end-systems, but not the underlying network). This would be by far too slow. There would be no Web!
- Another major advantage is that the routing is more dynamic as packets are independent, and the network may easily adapt to changing conditions without impacting the service, as packet reroutes may remain unnoticed. Thus, the network appears as more resilient to failures.

  Conversely, connection-oriented networks have also advantages:
- Connection-oriented networks, being aware of the requests before conversations actually start, by means of the *connection set up* procedure, may better predict the traffic load.
- If the traffic is more predictable, *resources* may be *reserved* more easily.
- If not enough resources are available, then the connection is refused. This is called the "busy signal", the functionality by which the network tells the user *"Sorry, I can't accept you call for the moment, please try later"*. This is what we experience with the telephone network, the oldest connection-oriented service. This process is called *"Call Admission Control"* (*CAC*) or also *"Capacity Admission Control"* because what matters for deciding whether a new request for connection is granted is the available capacity of the network.
- It is therefore easier for connection-oriented networks to guarantee the quality of service of the communications they support.

3. Why improving Quality of Service?

The objective of the efforts undertaken since the beginning of the nineties about the Internet quality of service is to improve the predictability of the service. Indeed, the historical "best effort datagram service" results in a somewhat unpredictable behavior. There are multiple reasons why this has become no longer desirable:

- Users may wish to set up *Virtual Private Networks* (*VPN*) over the shared Internet with a guaranteed Quality of Service, such as the bandwidth of the pipes between sites that are part of the VPN. For example, imagine a company with one head-quarter and three branches, all four connected to the same *Internet Service Provider* (*ISP*) - to simplify the case. The VPN is to be made of three links between the branches and the head-quarters, each with a guaranteed bandwidth of say, 1 Megabit/second. Can we do that with the current Internet, that is with regular routers? No, we cannot. We need something more than the "best effort datagram service".
- Users which connect to an ISP at a given access speed may wish to have a secure aggregate bandwidth out of this access link, irrespective of the destination of their traffic. For example, a company connecting to an ISP at 1.5 Megabit/second, and thus paying for that access speed, may wish to be guaranteed at least 2/3 of this access bandwidth for all its outgoing traffic, wherever it goes. Again, we cannot do this with the "best effort datagram service".
- More and more multimedia applications use the Internet, in particular, audio and video streams. These streams usually need a minimum bit rate, below which it makes no sense to try and send the audio or video traffic. These are requirements that do not apply to aggregates of traffic as in the above case, but to point-to-point flows between two end-systems.

4. Service Discrimination

Thus, the efforts for improving the *Quality of Service* (*QoS*) guarantees aim at moving away from the historical model of traffic where all packets are handled with the same priority by the network. By abandoning the pure egalitarian treatment of the datagrams, the new Quality of Service techniques create discrimination between packets. This is called *service discrimination.*

Service discrimination does not create any resource by itself -we do not get more bit rate on a link because some packets have higher priorities- therefore, it is not solving all problems of

Quality of Service. If a network, or a portion of a network (a link), has not enough capacity, service discrimination will not help for all the traffic. However it will help for some. Indeed, the objective of service discrimination is to give better service to some traffic. But this is done at the expense of giving a worse service to the rest. Hopefully, this only occurs in *times of congestion.*

In passing, this move from an egalitarian world, where all packets were equal, to a world where some packets are "more equal than others", a world where discrimination is legalized or organized, was viewed by some as orthogonal to the evolution of our society. We will leave this discussion to the judgement of the reader.

5. Integrated Services

The first substantial work on Quality of Service in the Internet started in the early nineties in the framework of what was called the *Integrated Services* (*IS*) model. The first release was made in 1993.

The Integrated Services model is based on the statement that a single *class* of packets is no longer sufficient, and that new classes with higher priorities are needed, in the same way as we have the economy, business and often first class with airlines. How many new classes were needed? The Integrated Services model opted for two new classes of packets, resulting in a total of three possible classes in the new discriminated Internet world:

- The *best effort service class* (*BE*)

  This is the default class
- The *controlled-load service class* (*CS*)

  There, if the sender respects a certain traffic profile (that is a certain bit rate) for a given flow, then the network promises to behave as though it was *unloaded*, but without *quantitative* guarantees in particular of the latencies of the packets.
- The *guaranteed service class* (*GS*)

  In this case, packets are promised to be delivered within a *firmly bounded delay*. This is for special applications with very stringent time delivery requirements.

6. Resource Reservations

The guiding principles of the Integrated Services model are the following:

- **Resource reservation is necessary**

To improve the guarantees, the key resources needed in the network must be *reserved* in some way.

- **Reservations operate on flows**

A *flow* is a stream of packets between a source and a destination (note that the destination may be a unique destination in the usual cases, but also a multiple destination, in case of a multicast flow; but this is comment for the specialists). For every flow that needs to benefit from either the *CS* or the *GS* service, reservations need be made.

- **Routers have to maintain flow-specific states**

By *state*, we mean a block of memory in the router where information about the flow and its requirements are stored: the service class (*CS* or *GS*), the bit rate to guarantee for that flow, the conditions for delay if applicable.

- **Dynamic Reservations need a signaling (set-up) protocol**

This protocol has been specified and is called *Resource Reservation Protocol*, or *RSVP*.

7. How to express Quality of Service?

For a given flow, the *parameters* for determining the Quality of Service belong to two groups. The two groups reflect a *contract* between the user of the network on the one hand - or more exactly the user *sending* the traffic - and the network on the other hand.

- **Traffic parameters**

The first group specifies what the flow *traffic pattern* is to be: parameters include the *sustained bit rate*, and the *burst size*, that is the tolerance that exists for the sender to exceed for short periods of time the sustained bit rate - as long as over longer periods, the average bit rate remains within the limit of the sustained bit rate.

The sender promises in the contract to respect this traffic profile.

- **Quality parameters**

These parameters specify the quality the network promises in turn to guarantee if the sender respects its agreed traffic profile. There are two things the network can possibly promise:

- *latencies*, that is guarantees on the delay it takes for packets to traverse the network; this is called the *transit delay*

- *loss ratio*: that the maximum proportion of packets not delivered against the total number of packets sent.

8. RSVP Guiding Principles

The *Resource Reservation Protocol, RSVP,* is the mechanism defined by the Integrated Services for reserving resources in the network. It is called a *signaling* protocol, because its aim is to *signal* to the network that a given flow is going to require certain guarantees for latencies and loss ratio, if the flow respects a certain bit rate. RSVP is based on a number of guiding principles.

- **RSVP is to co-exist with regular datagram service**

Any router which supports RSVP, also supports the regular best effort datagram service.

- **RSVP does not set hard connections**

Instead, the connections are said to be "soft" (a concept explained a bit later).

- **The amount of reserved resources is recipient driven**

That is, the sender will only *propose* a certain traffic profile. But this is the receiver system which will *decide* how much of this proposed bit rate it can accommodate. Indeed, a frequent case may be when the sender is a fast powerful server system and the receiver a slow desktop device. The capabilities of the receiver to process the received data, for example to decompress a video stream, may be much lower than that of the sending server.

- **Reservations are unidirectional**

If an application requires bi-directional reservations (such as in telephony, which is of course different from viewing a movie over the Internet, which is one-way only application), two reservations will have to be made, one in every direction.

9. RSVP Protocol Mechanisms

The RSVP protocol is only concerned with conveying information - along a path followed by a flow - to routers so that they can reserve the resources they need. For this, the protocol uses special RSVP *control packets*, which are packets which will be recognized by *RSVP-aware routers* and treated as such. The two main RSVP control packets are the *PATH* message and the *RESV* (reservation) message. The mechanisms for reserving resources for a given flow between a sender and a receiver are as follows:

- The "PATH" control messages are to be sent periodically by the sender. This message carries the traffic parameters and the details of the requested service class. It has to be repeated periodically (thus, the sender keeps "saying" to the network "*I still need this quality of service for that particular flow*").
- The "PATH" control messages establishes an RSVP state in the intermediary routers
- The receiver replies with a "RESV" message, according to its capabilities
- The "RESV" message reserves resources, if available, in routers on the route back.
- I not enough resource are available at a given router, the router generates an error control message to the end-systems.
- If "PATH" is not repeated after time-out, then the resources are released
- "PATH" and "RESV" messages are carried by ordinary best-effort datagrams

10. Which Resources are Reserved

One aspect of RSVP which may be surprising at first sight is that the protocol which aims at reserving resource does not define what those resources are. And there is a good reason for this. The "resources", that is "what is important" for a router or for a given transmission medium between two routers to guarantee a certain performance is fully implementation dependent. In particular, RSVP makes no assumption on the internals of routers.

That being said, in practice, with today's routers and transmission links, reservations generally apply to two types of resources:

- a slice of the link bandwidth
- a fraction of the buffers from the buffer pool of the routers

Note that *reservation* is different from *allocation*. Reserving means that a given amount has been secured for a flow, but the exact and precise resource is not allocated (yet). This is similar to reservation in public transportation networks: reserving a flight ticket is different from getting the seat allocated.

11. Path Stability

A difficult problem with RSVP lies with the fact that resources are reserved for a given flow over a given path. This path is the one followed by the initial PATH and RESV messages.

However, it may turn out that the route followed by the packets change after the reservation has been made. This happens in particular if the route used for the first reservation was a long path, because a shorter path between the two end-systems was unavailable at that time (due to a router or link failure). When the shortest path is back to availability, the data will naturally take this shortest route because this is how the regular Internet routing works: packets always try and take the shortest route.

We then have the reservations made on the longer initial route and the data flowing on a new shortest route where no reservation has been made. Fortunately, the situation may clear itself after a while, because PATH messages are repeated (roughly every minute). The next repeated message will then take the shortest route and reserve resources on this new route.

This is unfortunately not a complete solution, because it may turn out that there are not enough resources available on the shortest route. Then, the two users experience a situation where, without knowing why, they move from a good quality transmission to a bad one, simply because rerouting took place. What we need for a more complete solution is a means of having more stability for reserved paths, but also for finding routes, possibly longer, but which do have the required resources when the shortest route can not satisfy a given request. Such a routing technique for not only finding a short route but also one with enough resources to satisfy a certain quality of service is called *Quality of Service-based routing.*

12. RSVP Overhead for Data Packets

Another difficulty with RSVP lies in the *overhead* created in every router by the need to analyze every packet in order to know which priority it has, or more exactly which *service class* it belongs to (Best effort, Controlled-load, Guaranteed).

The process of deciding which service class an incoming packet belongs to is called *classification*. In the case of RSVP, how can we know the class? Is there any mark somewhere in the packet header, any field than can be rapidly and easily examined and that would tell us: *"It is class 1, 2 or 3"?* The answer is no: the class is not explicitly stated in the data packets when using RSVP only.

By examining the pair of source and destination addresses (and possibly other fields such a the protocol type) that characterizes every flow and by looking at a table to check whether a reservation has been made for that particular pair, the router knows the class of the packet. This technique, which rely on the examination of *multiple fields* (at least two), is called *multi-field classification*. Multi-field classification, which is to be performed on every packet, creates serious overhead to RSVP routers.

13. RSVP Scalability

The overhead of packet classification is one of the drawback of RSVP and raises a scalability issue.

Another scalability difficulty lies in the fact that *states* -that is, a block of memory that stores static and dynamic information about the reservation - has to be created and maintained for every pair of sender and receiver that has to enjoy an improved service. If this may be appropriate for small scale Intranets with a limited number of concurrent RSVP reservations, the need to maintain states per individual flow is unsuitable for large scale Internets. This was the argument from opponents to RSVP, and this triggered the development of another, complementary technology called *DiffServ*, which is examined after the RSVP.

14. Summary of RSVP Deficiencies, and Ways of Overcoming Them

We have seen that RSVP, though being an effective mechanism for reserving resources has three shortcomings:

1. **The per-flow states to maintain in routers**

   This entails a scalability problem for large scale Internets.

2. **The multi-field classification on data packets**

   The overhead generated by the need to analyze every packet by examining multiple fields in order to determine the service class of that packet.

3. **The instability of routes and**
   the lack of quality of service-based routing

   The fact that resources are reserved along routes and that we cannot guarantee the data traffic will follow these routes.

We see in the next sections how three rather recent technologies can be associated to RSVP so as to overcome most of those deficiencies. These technologies are:

- *RSVP aggregation*, to overcome problem 1
- *Diffserv*, to overcome problem 2
- *MPLS*, to overcome problem 3

15. RSVP Aggregation

RSVP Aggregation is a recent technique not yet stabilized at the time of this writing but very promising. The aim is to drastically reduce the number of states to be maintained in the network. This is a technology to be used within the core of the large scale Internet networks, not a technology for Intranets or limited scale Internets. The idea is to replace the reservations made per individual flow in the plain RSVP, by reservations made for aggregates of flows. Which aggregates?

Simply consider the core of a network and imagine that this core uses RSVP aggregation, that is, all the routers in the core understand the RSVP aggregation protocol. This core is made of a number of routers, some of them being *edge routers* - that is, having connection to the "non-RSVP aggregation" periphery - and others being *interior routers* only. The idea is that for any pair of edge routers, a *single* reservation will be made for all the flows that enter the core through one router of the pair and that exit the core through the other router of the pair. Thus, all those flows with the same *ingress* and *egress* router will share the same reserved path, and the amount of resources reserved over that path will match the sum of the individual requirements (not necessarily exactly).

As a result, if there are N edge routers surrounding the RSVP aggregation core, we will have (N^2-N) paths, therefore states, to maintain (remember, the reservation are unidirectional, thus we need two paths per pair in practice). This may be a big number but anyway lower than the total number of individual flows aggregated within the reserved paths.

16. Diffserv

Diffserv, which stands for *Differentiated Services*, is another recent technique aiming at overcoming the problem of heavy classification - that is the process for routers of knowing which service class a packet belongs to. The idea it to "mark" the packets with and indication of their priority in order to avoid having routers examining multiple fields. This mark is called a *"differentiated mark"*, or *a Diffserv Code Point* (*DSCP*) and serves to map to a *differentiated treatment* to be applied to the packet. For a fast classification, the "mark" must be:

- of fixed length
- located at the beginning of the packet
- in a fixed position
- to be used as a direct pointer to find out what the differentiated treatment is to be.

The use of the mark is similar to that of RSVP aggregation: this is a technique which assumes that there is a core in the network which is *"Diffserv-capable"*, that is, made of routers which understand the Diffserv marks and know how to exploit them for efficiently determining the packet priority. At the *edge* of this Diffserv core, the edge routers must be provisioned with the appropriate instructions to mark the packets (e.g. based on identification of flows such as source and destination addresses)

Therefore, by combining in the core of the network, RSVP aggregation and Diffserv marking, we can overcome two of the deficiencies of the plain RSVP:

- RSVP aggregation reduces drastically the number of reservations to maintain
- Diffserv removes the overhead of CPU-consuming classification by providing a simple, fast way of knowing the packet priority.

The final technology we briefly examine, *MPLS*, will help us with the third difficulty, the route stability and the need for finding routes which also satisfy some quality of service constraints.

17. MPLS

MPLS stands for *Multi-Protocol Label Switching*. This is not a Quality of Service technique per se. This is a *forwarding* technology, a new approach to build network nodes which are neither pure IP routers nor pure switches, rather *hybrid* objects which try and combine the good points of both systems. The objective of MPLS is to build network nodes which can forward packets fast, hopefully at "hardware speed". More exactly, the technology provides a mechanism for making a fast *forwarding decision*, that is deciding to which outgoing link an incoming packet should be sent. To this end, MPLS uses a *logical reference*, called a *label*, which is inserted somewhere in the header of the packet. MPLS routers are provided with forwarding tables that map the incoming label to an outgoing link. The mechanism is analogous to the switching done in ATM or in X.25 switches.

MPLS, as RSVP aggregation and Diffserv, uses the *core* and *edge* principle. The MPLS technology is used within an *"MPLS-capable"* core, a mesh of MPLS routers. When entering the core, all packets taking the same route receive the same label, which is then used within the core by routers to take the forwarding decision, instead of the destination address as done outside the MPLS core.

This technique is not per se a solution to the remaining difficulty of the plain RSVP: the route stability and the Quality of Service-based Routing. However, it turns out that the paths followed by all the packet which carry the same label (called *LSPs*, *Label Switched Paths*) may be *constrained* to have a certain *stability* (for example, only change in case of failure), or to match certain *performance* characteristics such as securing a certain bit rate or transit delay. The later facility, *called constraint-based routing* is nothing else than a form of Quality of Service-based Routing.

18. Conclusion

The combination of three techniques to be used in the core of large scale Internet:

- RSVP aggregation for reserving resources, yet limiting the number of states to maintain,
- Diffserv for a fast and easy classification of the data packets into service classes, and
- MPLS for providing appropriate route stability and Quality of Service-based Routing

is likely to provide in the future a solution which supports Quality of Service and is scalable.

References

[1] Understanding Network Multimedia, François Fluckiger, Prentice Hall, ISBN: 0-13-190992-4

[2] Quality of Service in IP Networks, Grenville Armitage, MacMillan Technical Publishing, ISBN: 1-57870-189-9

[3] MPLS, Technology and Applications, Bruce Davie and Yakov Rekhter, Morgan Kaufmann

[4] Interconnections Second Edition, Radia Perlman, Addison-Weisley, ISBN: 0-201-63448-1

Network Empowerment
O.B. Popov (Ed.)
IOS Press, 2004

Iskra Djonova-Popova and Oliver B. Popov

Congestion Control Strategies

1. Introduction

In the early days of the Internet, the main concern was to get an access to the global network, to enlarge the number of users, as well as to enable sharing of the accumulated knowledge distributed on various sites. Indeed, the interest was focused on connecting networking devices, the choice of technology to be implemented, the configuration of hosts and routers, and staff and user training. With the rapid development of networking infrastructure, inter alia, a need arouse to take preventive measures for an effective and fair resource allocation among the competing users in order to avoid the network entering a state of congestion. The control of the network resources is based on many networking concepts such as the nature of the data flow, quality of service, congestion or resource allocation. While of all these notions are very much interdependent and are used oftent interchangeably, the intention of the paper is to explain what is usually understood by congestion, and give a brief survey of the mechanisms for controlling this phenomenon in a TCP/IP environment.

2. From Flow Control to Quality of Service

When two devices are communicating directly, via a single transmission link, the sender can transmit more data than the receiver is able to process. Flow control is used by the receiver to throttle the sender. Various sliding window schemes, based on feedback mechanisms, are deployed to implement the flow control. Naturally, the limitations on the flow can be imposed when the sender and the receiver are connected via a many transmission links. However, the flow control in this case is still concerned with the buffers availability at the receiver and the transmission speed of the sender.

The occurrence of congestion is a consequence of the dynamically shared resources in the network. It includes the bandwidth of the links and the buffers of the routers or switches where packets are queued awaiting transmission. Packets contend at the router for the use of the link. Each packet placed in the queue is waiting for its turn to be transmitted over the link. When too many packets enter the competition for the same link and the number of buffers is scarce, some packets have to be dropped. If this happens often, the network is said to be congested. Therefore, congestion control mechanisms are used to prevent and to deal with the occurrence of this undesirable situation.

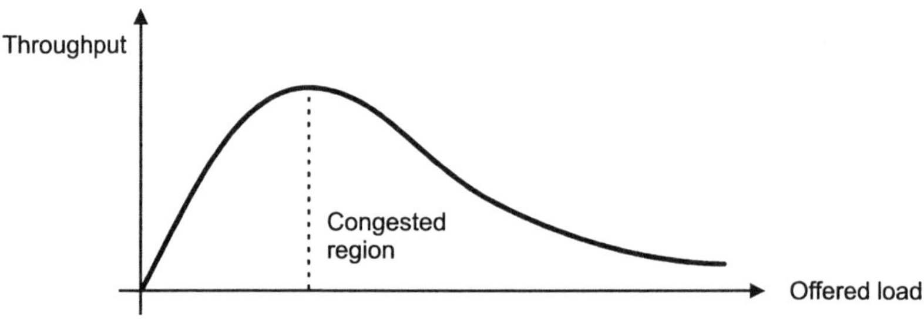

Figure 1a

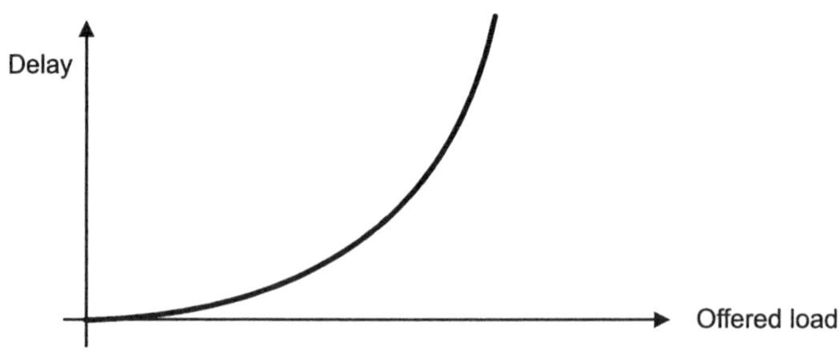

Figure 1b

Whenever there many packets are in the network and no congestion control mechanisms exist, the network might easily reach a congested state. After a while, a total collapse of the network becomes a reality, as depicted on the diagrams in Figure 1a and 1b. The first one shows the total throughput in the network while the second one represents the delay. When the number of packets dropped is within the normal operational capacity of the network, the overall throughput is proportional to the offered load and the total delay is small. As traffic increases close or beyond the capacity, the routers are no longer able to cope with the load and begin loosing packets. The lost packets need to be retransmitted. This in turn will increase the traffic even more and make the situation even worse. When the traffic becomes very high, performance collapses completely, and packet delivery approaches zero. At the same time the delay increases infinitely.

Figure 2 shows the throughput versus offered load diagram in three different situations with respect to the control: an ideal one, the absence of and the presence of congestion controlled environment.

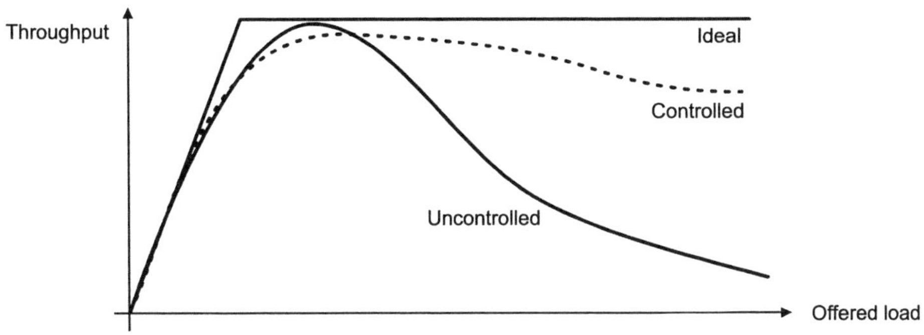

Figure 2

The essential difference between flow and congestion control is that while the first keeps the fast sender from overrunning the slow receiver, the second keeps the set of senders from sending too much data into the network because of lack of resources at some point.

Congestion control and resource allocation are two sides of the same coin. Namely, if the network takes an active role in allocating resources than congestion control can become unnecessary. Nevertheless, allocating network resources in a correct manner in a dynamically shared packet switched network is a difficult task. It cannot be easily achieved without affecting the flexibility in sharing and the effectiveness in using network resources. If the load increases in one part of the network, a good routing algorithm can redistribute it over less busy part of the network. By choosing alternative routing paths, the congestion can be only delayed. If the load increase is not prevented, entering the congested region becomes inevitable.

In addition to flow control, congestion control and resource allocation, another concept such as quality of service is entertained frequently. Quality of service discussion currently embraces many abstract concepts and varying ideologies. Moreover, these discussions occasionally lack a unified definition on what quality of service actually is and how it might be implemented.

The Internet historically has offered a single level of service known as the "best effort", where all data packets are treated equally. The Internet itself does not offer a single level of service quality. Some areas of the network exhibit excessive congestion and consequently poor service quality, while other areas display consistent levels of high quality of service. There are a number of characteristics that determine quality of service like minimizing delivery delay and its variations (jitter), and providing consistent data throughput capacity.

The new breed of applications, including audio and video streaming, demand high bandwidth and have low-latency requirements when used in two-way communications (i.e. conferencing and telephony). Unlike "pure virtual circuit" technologies like ATM and Frame Relay, the Internet does not make hard allocations of resources. While this provides more flexible and efficient use of the available bandwidth, it also leads to some unpredictability in service that especially affects new applications. There has been an intensive research dealing with various policies intented to meet the requirements for certain quality of service in periods of congestion.

The paper is not about these policies. The emphasis is rather on understanding the problems caused by overload, the resulting congestion, and the mechanisms for its control in the Internet.

3. Network Overload and Congestion

Congestion can be caused by several factors. When a stream of packets is arriving on three or four input lines and all need the same output line, it is very likely that a queue will build up. If there is an insufficient number of buffers andor they are small, some packets will be lost. Adding more buffers may help up to a point, but it is not a complete remedy for the proble. Namely, Nagle discovered that in routers with an infinite of memory, congestion gets worse, not better [2]. The reason behind this is that by the time packets get to the front of the queue, they have already timed out and duplicates have been sent. Then all the packets will be duly forwarded to the next router, increasing the load all the way to the destination.

Unpleasant effects can be observed firstly because of the overload, and secondly due to the wastage of resources. In the example on Figure 3a, the packets from node A to node A′ are sent at constant speed of 0.8 units/s, while the rate of packets from node B to B′, λ units/s, increases linearly. As this rate reaches the value of 1, the buffers in node C start being monopolized by the packets from node B that are arriving 10 times faster than the packets from node A. The results in the decrease of total throughput in the simple network are shown on Figure 3b.

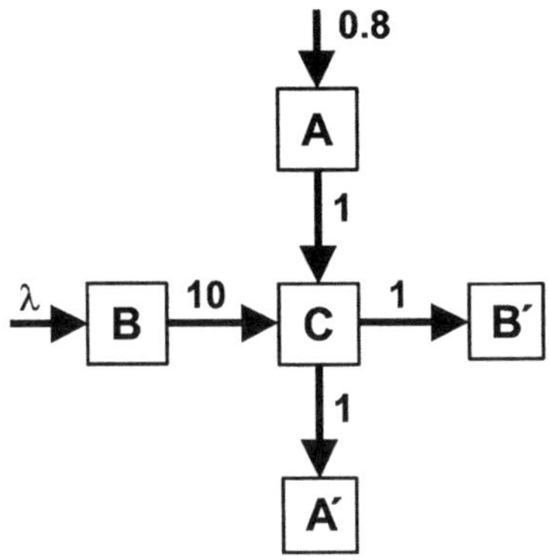

Figure 3a

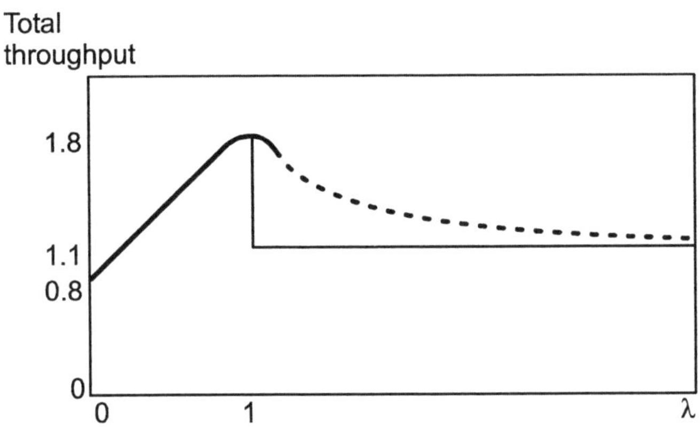

Figure 3b

Uncontrolled competition produces unfairness in using network resources among competing users.

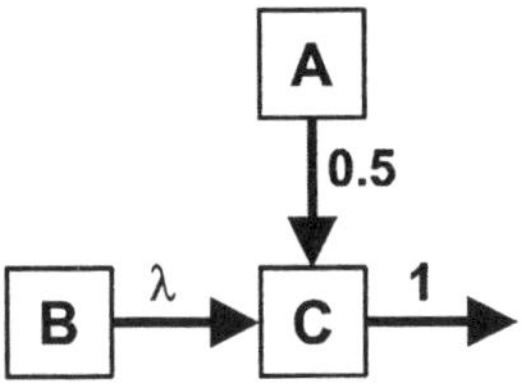

Figure 4a

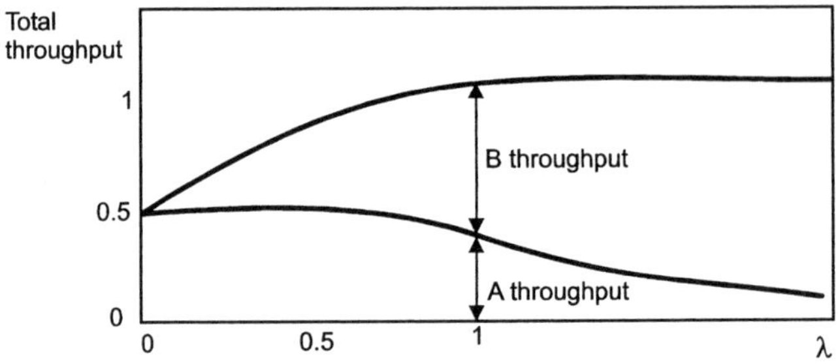

Figure 4b

Some users can obtain preferential treatment due to the relative position in the network or a particular selection of network and traffic parameters. The example in Figure 4 shows the consequences of the unfairness among A and B in using the buffers in node C.

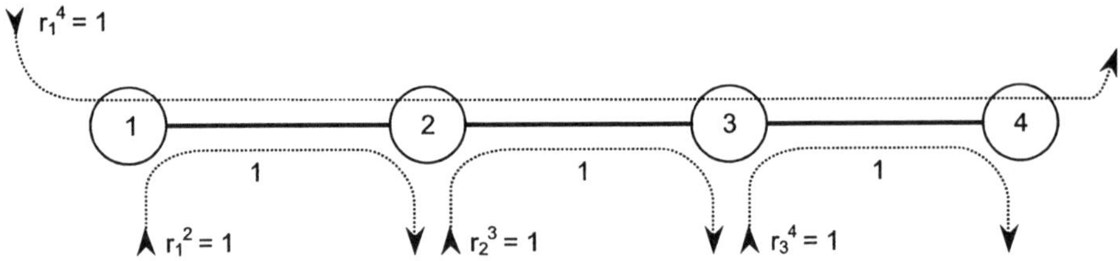

Figure 5

In Figure 5, the 3-hop flow from 1 to 4 competes with three one-hop flows. When all the links are fully utilized the four-hop flow is completely blocked. On the other side if all the flows are assigned a rate of 0.5 units/s, the total throughput will decrease from 3 units/s to 2 units/s.

The inconsistencies in routing tables can also cause an unwarranted overload in the network and lead to deadlocks.

4. Evaluation Criteria in Resource Allocation

A good starting point for evaluating the effectiveness of a resource allocation scheme is to consider the two principle metrics: throughput and delay. Clearly, it is desirable to have as much throughput and as little delay as possible. Basically, increasing the number of packets in the network in order to drive utilization of all the links up to 100% will increase the length of the queues at each router. Longer queues will cause longer delays for each packet, thus increasing the average delay in the network.

The ratio of throughput to delay is used as a metric for evaluating the effectiveness of resource allocation scheme. This ratio is sometimes referred as the power of the network.

$$\text{Power} = \text{Throughput}^{\alpha} / \text{Delay}$$

where $0 < \alpha < 1$. When $\alpha = 1$ the power is being maximized and corresponds to the point at the knee of the delay curve (Figure 1a).

Another important issue in allocating the resources is the fair sharing of the bandwidth. Assuming that fair implies equal and that all paths are of equal length, Raj Jain [2] has proposed a metric that can be used to quantify the fairness of the congestion control mechanism. Jain's fairness index is defined as follows. Given a set of flow throughputs $(x_1, x_2, x_3, \ldots, x_n)$ measured in consistent units such as bits/sec, the following function defines a fairness index for these flows:

$$f(x_1, x_2, x_3, \ldots, x_n) = (\Sigma_{i=1}^{n} x_i)^2 / n \, \Sigma_{i=1}^{n} x_i^2$$

The fairness index always results in a number between 0 and 1, with 1 representing greatest fairness. To understand the intuition behind this metric, consider the case where all n flows receive a throughput of 1unit/sec. In this case the index of fairness is $n^2/(n \times n) = 1$. Another simple case to consider is the case where only k out of n flows receive equal throughput, and the remaining (n-k) users receive zero throughput. In this case the index drops to k/n.

5. Handling Congestion

Two large groups of schemes can be distinguished with respect to congestion: mechanisms that deal with congestion avoidance versus congestion recovery mechanisms. The former group is preventive, while the latter one is reactive in nature.

There are mechanisms that avoid congestion and can be considered as reservation-based systems. In such a system the host asks the network for a certain amount of capacity at the time a flow is established. Each router then allocates enough resources (buffers and bandwidth) to satisfy this request. If some router declines to honor a request because doing so would mean over commitment of its resources, then the router rejects the flow. When there is no an alternative router the entire flow needs to be canceled.

In a network with this kind of policy, the congestion should not appear. However, in most of the networks today, especially the Internet, are not adequate to implement this kind of mechanism.

In the congestion avoidance schemes, the end hosts begin sending data without first reserving any capacity. Then, they will adjust their sending rate appropriately to the feedback they receive. This feedback can either be explicit (i. e. the congested router sends an explicit congestion notification to the host to make it slow down) or it can be implicit (i. e. the end host adjusts its sending rate to respond to the externally observable behavior of the network, such as packet losses).

Another way of classifying the resource allocation mechanisms is to distinguish two broad groups depending on the place where a particular scheme addresses the problem: from inside the network (i. e. at the routers or switches) or from the edges of the network (i. e. in the hosts). The former are referred to as router-centric and the later as host-centric procedures.

In a router-centric design, each router takes responsibility for deciding when packets are forwarded and which packets are dropped, as well as for informing the hosts that are generating the network traffic how many packets they are allowed to send. In a host centric design, the end hosts observe the network conditions to adjust their behavior.

The third way to categorize congestion mechanisms is based on the parameter they need to control the window or the rate. In the window based schemes, the window corresponds to the number of unacknowledged packets that can be sent and its size can vary depending on the load in the network. The same window mechanisms can be used for flow control, too. Another way to control the sender's behavior is to limit its sending rate. Rate-based control is a logical choice of the reservation based systems that support different quality of service such as ATM.

6. Congestion Control on the Internet

Source Quench and RED (Random Early Detection)

The oldest and fairly rudimentary method of detecting congestion in the routers has been to send an ICMP message (a source quench) to the host whenever a packet sent by that host is dropped. Today, source quench messages are rarely used, because they can consume network bandwidth in times of congestion. The reliance on packet drops as the indication of congestion is well suited for a network with routers whose function is to route packets to the appropriate output port. Most current routers in TCP/IP networks have no provision for the detection of incipient congestion. Future routers are likely to have more diverse and sophisticated mechanisms for congestion anticipation.

The DNA (Digital Network Architecture) was the first network technology to implement a mechanism for early detection of congestion. This was done by setting a binary congestion bit in the packets that flow through the router. That is where the name name DECbit came from. The destination host copies the congestion bit into the ACK it sends back to the source. Finally, the source adjusts its sending rate so as to avoid congestion.

Random Early Detection (RED) mechanism works similarly to the DECbit scheme. Namely, each router is programmed to monitor its own queue. When it detects that congestion is imminent, it notifies the source to adjust its congestion window. RED is commonly implemented in such a way that it implicitly notifies the source of congestion by dropping one of its packets. It is designed to be used in conjunction with TCP that commonly detects congestion by means of timeouts. The source is therefore effectively notified by the subsequent timeout or duplicate ACK. As the "early" part of the RED suggests, the gateway drops the packet earlier than it would have to, so as to notify the source that it should decrease its congestion window sooner than it would normally have. In other words, the router drops a few packets before it has exhausted its buffer space completely, so as to cause the source to slow down, with the hope that this will mean that it will not have to drop lots of packets later on.

Queuing disciplines

Packets from various sources enter the router so they can be processed and forwarded in the direction of their destination. When the link is busy, the packets are queued for transmission at the output buffers associated with the link. The queuing or scheduling discipline describes the manner in which the queued packets are selected for transmission on the link. If there is not sufficient buffering space to hold the arriving packet, the packet discarding policy of the queue determines the fate of the packet, that is being kept or dropped to make place for another arriving packet. When the packet is completely transmitted over the outgoing link, it is removed from the queue.

The FIFO (First In First Out) scheduling discipline selects packets for link transmission in the same order in which they arrive. When FIFO is used, the packet at the tail is usually the one that is dropped in case of buffer space shortage. FIFO with tail drop, as the simplest of all queuing algorithms, is the most widely used in the Internet routers.

A simple variation on basic FIFO is priority queuing. Under priority queuing, packets arriving at the output link are classified into one or more priority classes at the output queue. The classification is based on a marker carried in the packet (for example in the the IPthere is a Type of Service (TOS) field). Each priority class has its own queue. When choosing a packet for transmission, the priority queuing discipline will send a packet from the highest priority class that has a nonempty queue. The choice among packets in the same priority class is done in the FIFO manner.

The problem with priority queuing is that the high priority queue can starve out all the other queues. One obvious way to deal with this problem is to impose a higher charge for the delivery of high priority packets than low priority packets. There are significant challenges to implementing such a scheme in a decentralized environment such as the Internet. One situation in which priority queuing is used in the Internet is to protect the most critical packets. These are typically the routing updates that are necessary to stabilize the routing tables after a topology change.

When FIFO queuing is used, the entire congestion control mechanism is implemented at the sources. In case of the Internet these procedures are part of TCP. Naturally, it is possible for an application to use UDP, as a transport protocol, instead of TCP. The usage of UDP might flood the routers with its own packets, thereby causing other packets to be discarded.

Fair queuing or round robin is an algorithm that has been proposed to address this problem. Here the packets are again sorted in classes, as with priority queuing, but the router services these queues in a round robin manner, starting with the highest and ending with the lowest class. When a queue reaches a particular length, additional packets coming to that queue are discarded. In this way, a given source cannot arbitrarily increase its share of the capacity at the expense of other flows. A generalized abstraction of fair queuing or round robin queuing that has found considerable use, is the so called weighted fair queuing discipline. Weighted fair queuing differs from fair queuing in that each class may receive a differential amount of service in any interval of time. Specifically, each class, i, is assigned a weight w_i. Under weighted fair queuing, during any interval of time during which there are class i packets to send, class i will then be guaranteed to receive a fraction of service equal to $w_i/(Sw_j)$, where the sum in the denominator is taken over all classes that also have packets queued for transmission. In the worst case, even if all classes have queued packets, class i will still be guaranteed a fraction to $w_i/(Sw_j)$ of the bandwidth. The size of the fraction of the bandwidth for each class will depend on the weight assigned to it. The weights can be assigned either by manual configuration, or by some sort of signaling from the sources. In both cases the assignment of these weights should reflect the policy for resource allocation in the network.

Congestion Control Scheme in TCP

The predominant congestion control mechanism in the Internet is the "congestion avoidance" algorithm by Van Jacobson [5]. The algorithm became an integral part of TCP in the late 1980s. The idea behind the algorithm is for each source to determine how much capacity is available in the network, so that it knows how many packets it can safely have in transit. Once a given source has this many packets in transit, it uses the arrival or ACK as a signal that one of the packets has left the network, and that is therefore safe to insert a new packet into the network without adding to the level of congestion (packet conservation principle). Determining the available capacity is not an easy task. Since other connections come and go, the available bandwidth changes over time, meaning that any given source must adjust the number of packets it has in transit.

When a host starts a TCP connection, it has no idea of how many packets it is going to be able to have in transit. To avoid overloading the network, the TCP congestion control algorithm allows at most one unacknowledged packet to enter the network, regardless of the size of the receiver window. This is termed as "the slow start" phase. Each time an acknowledgement is received, it will increase that limit by one, which effectively doubles the congestion window every RTT (Round Trip Time). The periodic doubling results in an exponential increase of the transmission rate and should not be continued indefinitely, as it would congest the network. It ceases either when it notice a packet loss, in which case it resets the mechanism and starts from the beginning, or when it reaches a certain threshold, at which point it starts using linear increments, adding one packet to the window for every acknowledgement. Even linear increase will eventually lead to congestion, which will trigger the loss of a packet.

Congestion may result from other causes. These include but are not limited to an increase in network usage or a change in the routing towards a narrower backup channel. TCP plays it safely by immediately backing off to the minimal window of one packet. It will than begin the slow start procedure. Before backing off it will note the throughput or rather the congestion window that was in use at the time of congestion. The value of the new threshold for switching from the exponential to the linear phase will be one half of the current congestion window.

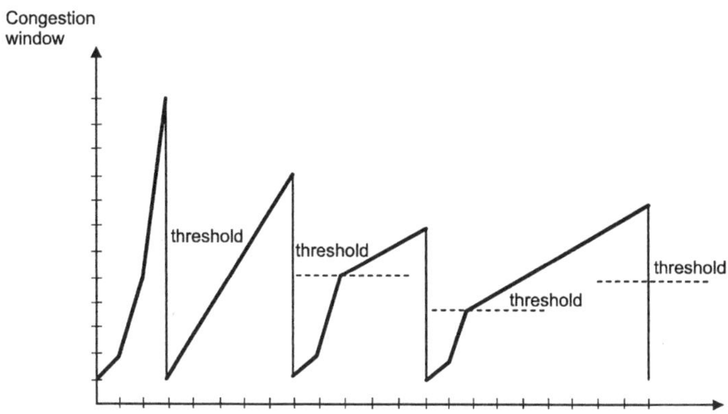

Figure 6

Figure 6 illustrates the congestion control scheme. If the slow-start phase is ignored, the TCP essentially increases its window size by 1 each RTT and thus increases its transmission rate by an additive factor when its path is not congested. However, it decreases its window size by a factor of 2 each RTT when its path is congested. Therefore, TCP's congestion control scheme is also referred to as an Additive-Increase, Multiplicative-Decrease (AIMD) algorithm.

A TCP congestion control algorithm, just described, is often referred to as Tahoe. The problem with the Tahoe algorithm is that, when a packet is lost, the sender may have to wait long time for the timeout in case some packet is being lost. During this time packets are not sent by the sender. To make this time shorter, a variant called Reno includes a fast retransmit mechanism that triggers the retransmission of a dropped packet. The sender retransmits the packet after three duplicate ACKs for the same data are received. The rationale behind this proposal is as follows. When a TCP receiver receives a segment with a sequence number that is larger than the next expected in order sequence number, it detects a gap in the stream, which equals to a missing segment. Since TCP does not use negative acknowledgements, the receiver cannot send an explicit negative acknowledgement back to the sender. Instead, it simply re-acknowledges the previous segment by generating a duplicate ACK. If the TCP sender receives three duplicate ACKs for the same data, it takes that as an indication that the segment following the segment that has been acknowledged three times has been lost and retransmits the missing segment before the segment's timer expires. Reno employees a fast-recovery mechanism that essentially cancels the slow-start phase after the fast retransmission.

Two other algorithms, DUAL and Vegas, propose changes to the algorithm in the sense that they both try to predict congestion without having to wait the packet to be dropped.

DUAL checks if the current RTT is greater than the previous RTT and if that is the case, it reduces the congestion window by 7/8. In this way DUAL tries to delay or completely avoid packets being dropped. The other variant, known as Vegas algorithm, attempts to avoid congestion, while maintaining good throughput. The basic ideas behind Vegas are:

- to detect congestion in the routers between source and destination before packet loss occur, and
- to lower the rate linearly when an imminent packet loss is detected, increase the rate whenever it is possible and keep it the same when the throughput is satisfactory.

By observing the round-trip times, two distinct thresholds defined. The first corresponds to having too little and the second to having too much "extra data" in the network. By "extra data" we mean data that the source would not have transmitted had it been trying to match exactly the available bandwidth of the network. If the current RTT is below the first threshold, TCP Vegas increases congestion window. If it is above the second threshold, the window is decreased, while for the values in between the two thresholds, the congestion window remains unchanged. TCP Vegas increases and decreases the congestion window linearly. Linear decrease is in conflict with the rule for multiplicative decrease, needed to ensure stability. TCP Vegas does use multiplicative decrease when a timeout occurs. The linear decrease in reality is just an early decrease in the congestion window. It takes place before actual congestion occurs and packets start being dropped.

7. Conclusion

The congestion control is an important issue. The reason behind this is its important task to prevent the overall degradation of service when there is a mismatch between the demand for resources and their availability. Most congestion control mechanisms in the Internet today are targeted at the best-effort service model. In this case the primary responsibility falls on the end nodes of the network. The source uses the feedback, either implicitly learned from the network or explicitly sent by a router, to adjust the load it places on the network. Independent of what the end nodes are doing, the routers implement queuing discipline that governs which packets get transmitted and which packets get dropped. Sometimes, these algorithms are sophisticated enough to segregate traffic. In other cases, the router attempts to monitor its queue length and then signal the source host when congestion is about to occur.

The ambitions of emerging Quality of Service notions and strategies go substantially beyond control congestion. Their goal is to enable applications with widely varying requirements for delay, loss and throughput to be addressed and resolved through mechanisms inside the network. The desired QoS in heterogeneous network environments is part of the intensive effort in an area of networking and the Internet, which most certainly includes congestion management.

References

[1] Larry C. Peterson & Bruce S. Davie, "Computer Networks", Academic Press, 2000.

[2] James F. Kurose & Keith W. Ross, "Computer Networking", Addison Wesley, 2001.

[3] Lawrence S. Brakmo and Sean W. O'Malley, "TCP Vegas: New Techniques for Congestion Detection and Avoidance," *SIGCOMM '94 Conference on Communications Architectures and Protocols*, (London, United Kingdom), pp. 24-35, Oct. 1994.

[4] Sally Floyd and Van Jacobson, "Random Early Detection Gateways for Congestion Avoidance," *IEEE/ACM Transactions on Networking*, vol. 1, pp. 397-413, Aug. 1993.

[5] Van Jacobson, "Congestion Avoidance and Control," *ACM Computer Communication Review*, vol. 18, pp. 314-329, Aug. 1988. *Proceedings of the Sigcomm '88 Symposium* in Stanford, CA, August, 1988.

[6] Zheng Wang and Jon Crowcroft, "Eliminating Periodic Packet Losses in the 4.3-Tahoe BSD TCP Congestion Control Algorithm," *ACM Computer Communication Review*, vol. 22, pp. 9-16, Apr. 1992.

Network Empowerment
O.B. Popov (Ed.)
IOS Press, 2004

Wolfgang Schneider

Security in Open Systems

1. Introduction

Computers and computer communication systems are increasingly used to store and exchange valuable assets, for instance to do real business over networks, to purchase goods or to transmit payment orders. In contrast to paperbound information where a number of independent physical features can be used to verify or falsify the authenticity of a document or to protect it from disclosure, digital information is immaterial. It can be observed or modified without leaving a trace. Additional measures are needed to protect the electronic data against accidental or intentional loss, alteration and misuse. In open systems like the Internet people often do not know each other, or they may have conflicting interests. Nevertheless they want to communicate in unlimited, spontaneous, perhaps anonymous, but a reliable way. People acting in the digital world need a similar level of assurance about their partner's identities, the integrity of information and protection of their privacy as they are used to have in the "real" world, including the possibility to use the legal system in case of conflicts.

We can observe basically four types of threats against information security in open networks that can be qualified as follows:

- Unauthorized release of information by passive observation.
- Unauthorized modification of information, i.e. changing, duplicating or replaying exchanged information between two entities.
- Masquerading in various forms.
- Repudiation of communication, both by the originator or the recipient of information.

Authenticity is the key issue of security. Authenticity of the subjects (persons, organizational instances, program instances, hardware components) and of the objects (information, files, programs, keys) of information processing systems is the basis where the transferability of responsibilities relies upon, which in turn is the basis of every kind of cooperative work. Security requirements such as integrity of data, access control, non-repudiation or prevention of masquerade (i.e. playing the role of others) can only be fulfilled if one is able to rely on authentic partner relations. Many open systems applications have security requirements, which depend upon correctly identifying the principles involved. Such requirements may include the protection of assets and resources against unauthorized access, for which an identity based access control mechanism might be used, and/or for accounting and charging purposes. The process of corroborating an identity is called authentication.

Confidentiality is an issue, too, for a number of applications. This is the classical playground of cryptography. Information which belongs to the privacy of people like personal data, medical data etc., or information which represent an economic asset for individuals or organizations, should not be transmitted in clear text over public networks if the disclosure of such information by unauthorized people could lead to economic or other damage. End-to-end encryption between the connected applications is essential in many cases, while encryption measures between network components are additional possibilities that might be useful to encounter traffic analysis and the like.

However, it should be noted that achieving confidentiality is not possible without authenticity. One has to be sure with whom to exchange or share keys for confidentiality purposes, otherwise encryption might not be of great value.

Access control. Many open systems applications have security requirements, which demand that resources be only used in a manner consistent with the prevailing security policy. The process of determining whether the use of resources within an open system environment is permitted and subsequently preventing such use is called access control.

Non-repudiation. The non-repudiation services ensures the proper collection and maintenance of information consisting of the origin or delivery of data in order to protect an originator against the false denial of a recipient that the data has been received or to protect a recipient against the false denial by an originator that the data has been sent.

Data Integrity. The maintenance of data value is actually its integrity. Many open system applications have security requirements, which depend upon the integrity of information. Such requirements may include the protection of information used in the provision of other security services such as authentication, access control, confidentiality, audit and non-repudiation, that, if an attacker could modify them could reduce or nullify the effectiveness of those services.

Audit. A security audit is an independent review and examination of system records and activities. The purpose of a security audit is an independent review and examination of system records and activities. The security audits: tests the adequacy of system controls, confirm compliance with established security policy, recommend any indicated changes in controls, policy and procedures, assists in the analysis of the attacks, and hence recommend damage control procedures. A security audit requires the collection and recording of security related events in a security audit trail. A security audit itself involves the analysis and reporting of the information collected by the security audit trail.

To summarize, we can observe a need for:

- **Authenticity**
  On the Internet, everyone is anonymous. Secure identification is indispensable for any kind of legally binding electronic transaction.

- **Integrity**
  Every digital transaction, which may lead to financial consequences, has to be protected from tampering or forgery.

- **Non-repudiation**
  Neither party involved in a digital transaction should be able to deny their action

- **Privacy**
  Users of open networks must be able to protect their privacy and to work in closed groups.

- **Support of the legal system**
  Electronic business or other forms of teleco-operation must be recognized by the legal system. A digital signature on an electronic document must be usable in a court with the same evidence as a written signature.

2. How it Works

The invention of public-key cryptography by Whitfield Diffie and Martin Hellman, and independently by Ralph Merkle in 1976, and the publication of the **RSA** public-key algorithm by Rivest, Shamir and Adleman in 1978 made all this possible. Public-key systems allow to create **digital signatures** which "seal" digital information together with an identification of its originator. Digital signatures are cryptographically computed checksums of the information to be signed. They are the basis of **Digital Ids** by which people can securely identify themselves in the digital world. Public-key systems also allow to securely transmit encryption keys for confidentiality purposes within open networks in a way that only the intended recipients are able to disclose the information, thus providing the means to create closed groups in open networks.

The fundamental means to provide authenticity and confidentiality is cryptography. Cryptographic algorithms are being used for two purposes. One is to prove to others that one is in the possession of a certain key. If the partner or verifier is able to decrypt information, which was previously encrypted using this key, the proof is provided. If it is assured by other means, in addition, that no other person or instance can be in possession of this key, the use of this key produces a link to the user of the key. This is the way authentication is done. The other is to use cryptography in order to conceal information, i.e. to avoid unauthorized disclo-sure of information. It is the classical application of cryptography that aims at achieving confidentiality.

We can distinguish two main categories of cryptographic algorithms. One category comprises the **symmetric** algorithms. In this case, two parties communicate using a single key for encryption and decryption and a commonly agreed symmetric algorithm. The key must be kept secret to anyone but the two communicating parties. Divulging the key means that anyone could encrypt and decrypt messages. The vital steps for the sender and receiver are to agree on a key and to keep this key secret. Hence, the two main problems encountered in symmetric cryptography are:

- Key distribution, i.e. creating a key and distributing it to the corresponding communicating parties in secret.
- Key management which denotes the complexity of managing a separate key for each pair of communicating parties. In a network of n users $n(n-1)/2$ different keys are required.

Assuming that keys have not been compromised, symmetric cryptography provides for authenticity and integrity as well as confidentiality. The reason is that if one receives a message encrypted with a certain symmetric key, the message could have only been encrypted by the communication partner owning the corresponding key, if it has not been encrypted by oneself.

There are two categories of symmetric algorithms: *stream ciphers* and *block ciphers*. The first category operates on the plaintext a single bit at a time, the second operates on groups of bits, so-called blocks. A typical block size is 64 bits.

There are numerous symmetric algorithms, the best-known algorithms being DES, Triple DES, IDEA, RC2 and RC4. Typical key lengths for symmetric algorithms range between 40 bits (weak keys) and 128 bits (strong keys).

The best-known symmetric algorithm is the **Data Encryption Standard (DES)** invented 1977 by the American NBS (National Bureau of Standards, now NIST) and internationally standardized as DEA1 (Data Encryption Algorithm 1). The DES algorithm is a careful and complex combination of two of the fundamental building blocks of encryption: substitution and permutation. The algorithm derives strength from repeated application of these two techniques, one on top of the other, for a total of 16 cycles. Plaintext is encrypted as blocks of 64 bits. Although the key is 64 bits long, in effect the key can be any 56 bit number. The key can be changed by the user any time security of the old key may be uncertain. The algorithm uses only standard arithmetic and logical operations on up to 64-bit numbers, so it is suitable for software implementation on most current computers. Although complex, the algorithm is repetitive, making it suitable for implementation on a single-purpose chip. In fact, several such chips are available on the market for use as basic components in devices that use DES encryption in an application.

IDEA is another cryptosystem similar in the overall structure to DES. It derives its strength from the use of three different operations - exclusive OR, modular addition, and modular multiplication - in each round, rather than just using exclusive OR. Additionally it uses a 128 bit key to guard against exhaustive search attacks. The IDEA algorithm is patented, but the patent holders have granted blanket permission for non commercial use.

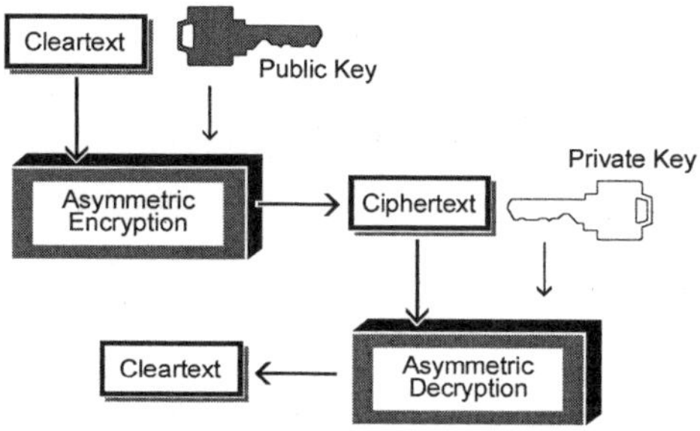

Figure 1. Asymmetric Encryption

The second category comprises the **asymmetric** algorithms. This type of algorithms uses different keys for encryption and corresponding decryption and was invented by Diffie and Hellmann in 1976. The two keys are mathematically dependent from each other, but it is a requirement to the algorithm that one key can be computed from the other key at most in one direction, while the other direction must be computationally infeasible. This one-way property allows to make one key (the one which can be derived from the other) public while the other key must be kept secret and unbreakably linked to a person or instance. Therefore this type of algorithm is also called **public key** algorithm.

The class of asymmetric algorithms can be subdivided into the two categories **reversible** public key algorithms and **irreversible** public key algorithms.

Reversible algorithms have also the property that applying the encryption function to a cleartext followed by applying the decryption function to the ciphertext results in the cleartext again and has the same effect as doing it in the reverse order, i. e. we have

$$d(e(cleartext, E), D) = e(d(cleartext, D), E) = cleartext$$

with ***e*** : encryption function
E : encryption key
d : decryption function
D : decryption key

This property allows to use a single algorithm and even a single key pair for both authentication/integrity and confidentiality purposes in that you use your own secret key to produce a digital signature which can be verified by everyone through your public key, and that another person uses your public key to send you information in a confidential way which you can decrypt using your secret key.

The best-known reversible asymmetric algorithm is the **RSA** algorithm invented by R. Rivest, A. Shamir and L. Adleman in 1978.

Irreversible asymmetric algorithms do not have this property, i.e. it is not possible with them to recover the cleartext from the ciphertext, and they don't have encryption / decryption functions in that sense. With them it is possible to verify with a public key component that a digital signature was produced with the corresponding private key component. Therefore, this type of algorithm is also called signature-only algorithm. The best known signature-only algorithms are the *ElGamal* algorithm invented by T. Elgamal in 1985, and the NIST variant of this algorithm, the **DSA** algorithm, used for the proposed US FIPS **Digital Signature Standard (DSS)**.

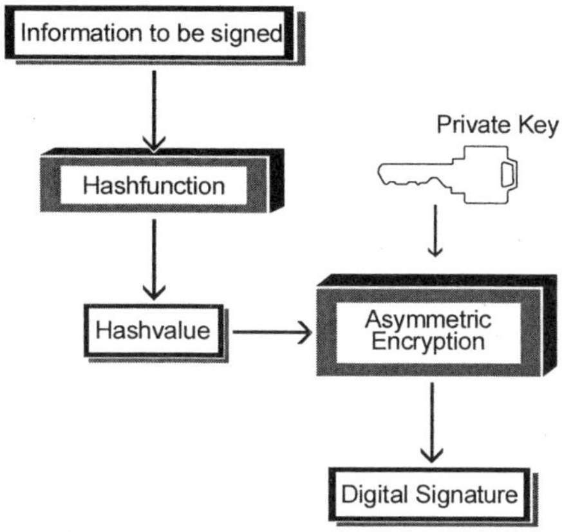

Figure 2. Generation of a Digital Signature

Another building block for digital signatures are **one-way hash functions.** A one-way hash function, *H(M)*, operates on an arbitrary-length pre-image message, *M*, and returns a fixed-length hash value, *h*.

One-way hash functions are used to produce a sufficiently unique fingerprint of digital information, i.e. very short representations of possibly large pieces of information, which nevertheless identify the original information without reasonable doubt. Fingerprints are useful for producing digital signatures of messages.

One-way hash functions must comply with the following characteristics in order to make them suitable for these purposes:

- Given *M*, it is easy to compute *h*
- Given *h*, it is impossible or at least hard to compute *M* such that *H(M)=h* (i.e. one-wayness)
- Given *M*, it is hard to find another message, *M'*, such that *H(M)=H(M')*

An even more far-reaching condition is the one of collision-resistance which means

- It is hard to find two random messages *M* and *M'* such that *H(M)=H(M')*

Symmetric algorithms can be realized very efficiently, but they have the problem of a shared secret. Two partners using symmetric cryptography must have the *same* secret key. This makes symmetric algorithms unsuitable for proving individual identities to third parties because at least two share the same key and the knowledge of the key doesn't provide a link to an individual user. Another problem is the necessity to transmit symmetric keys across networks if the communicating partners are on different places. Symmetric cryptography can be used for the purpose of authentication in conjunction with a central authentication server whom anyone trusts and which keeps the secrets of all partners.

The problem of the shared secret does not exist with asymmetric cryptography. Every person or instance, i.e. every subject, owns a unique *pair* of keys. One of them is to be published, while the access to the other must be unbreakably restricted to the subject itself through a secure local environment, e.g. a smartcard environment. By means of **digital signatures**, which are being generated through encrypting a hash value of the information to be signed using the private key, and which can be verified by everyone through decrypting the signature using the public key, authentic identifications and proofs of integrity can be exchanged in open systems. Confidentiality can be achieved, too, in the case of reversible algorithms (e.g. RSA) by encrypting the information with the recipient's public key. Everyone can do this, but only the recipient is able to decrypt the information with his secret key.

The application of asymmetric cryptography leads to a number of practical problems, also. One of them is that most known asymmetric algorithms rely on complex mathematical problems of number theory and the usage of very large integer numbers, which makes them considerably slower than symmetric algorithms.

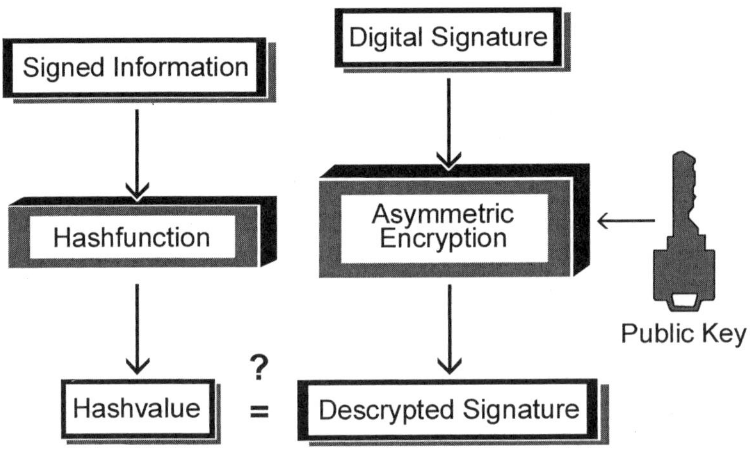

Figure 3. Verification of a Digital Signature

DES is about 1000 times faster than RSA. Asymmetric cryptography is not really suitable for the encryption of large amounts of data. A widely accepted solution is to encrypt data (for the purpose of confidentiality) using symmetric algorithms and to exchange the corresponding symmetric keys in encrypted form using reversible asymmetric algorithms. These so-called hybrid cryptosystems combine the best of both symmetric and public-key cryptosystems. Public-key algorithms are used for the distribution of keys for symmetric algorithms.

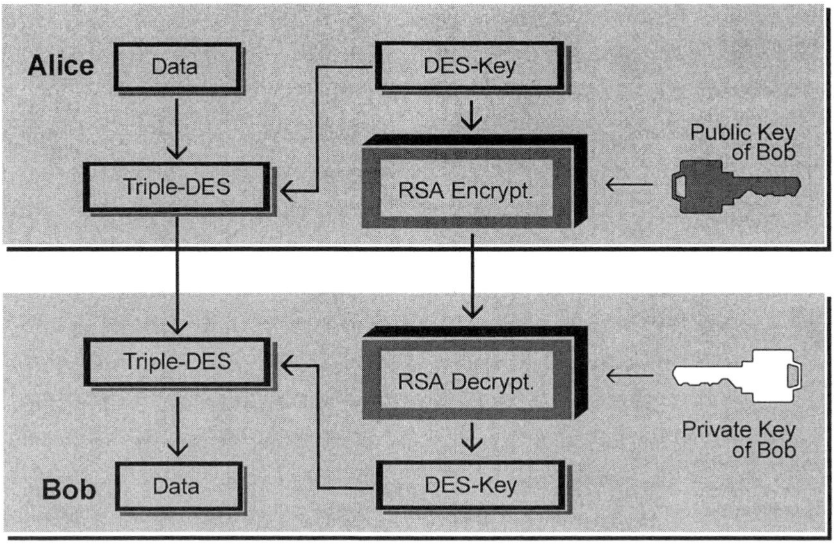

Figure 4. Hybrid Systems

3. Public Key Certification

A fundamental problem, which arises in open environments with large numbers of partners who do not know each other, is the question of the **authenticity of public keys**. At the time of verifying a digital signature the verifier must be sure that the public key, which he uses for the verification of the signature, is the public key of the supposed signer, i.e. he needs a key-to-name binding which he can trust.

Without additional measures each user would have to perform an out-of-band verification of the authenticity of each partner's public key before trusting it. Certifying public keys through a third party whom both signer and verifier trust can reduce the complexity of this problem. This third party, the so-called **certification authority** (CA), signs the user's public key and his name (plus some additional information such as a period of validity) with its own secret key. This piece of data, signed by the CA, is called a **certificate**. The certificate can be verified with the public key of the CA. Now two partners can authenticate each other by first verifying the partner's digital signature with the partner's public key and then verifying the authenticity of the partner's public key through verifying the digital signature of the certificate using the public key of the CA. Only the public key of the CA must be trusted, thus reducing the number of public keys to one that every user has to trust.

In large user populations representing perhaps millions of partners, a single CA is not sufficient. Other CAs may certify the public keys of certification authorities again. One can imagine tree structures of certification authorities, or network structures in that CAs belonging to different trees cross-certify each other, thus providing certification paths or chains of trust between individual partners.

However, the chain of certificates cannot be endless, and the public key in the last certificate remains uncertified. This is called the **Public Root Key,** which the user simply has to trust finally. The authenticity and integrity of this key has to be provided by out-of-band means. The key can be published, for instance, in a human readable form, and particular software may enable the user to compare this key with that what is stored in his computer. Once the public root key has been entered into the local computer system, its integrity must be protected by local means (for instance through the use of smartcards). The public root key, though public, is as security sensitive as the personal secret key. They are the two ends of the security chain between two individual partners.

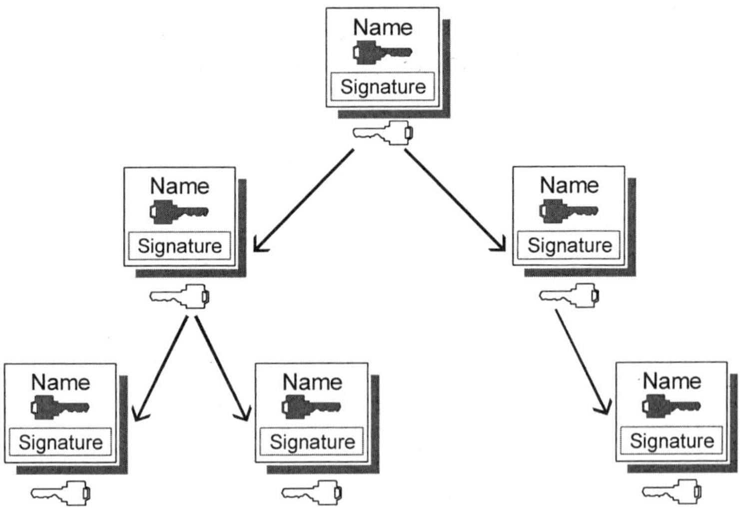

Figure 5. Certification of Public Keys

A CA must be able to revoke a certificate issued prior to its expiration time. There may be many reasons for a CA to revoke a certificate:

- The user's secret key is assumed to be compromised whereby the corresponding public component is invalidated.
- The user's affiliation has changed whereby the distinguished name contained in the certificate's 'subject' field is invalidated.

- The user is no longer to be certified by the CA.
- The CA's certificate is assumed to be compromised.
- The user has violated the CA's security policy.

A CA can mark on issued certificate as 'invalid' by adding it to the list of revoked certificates.

Information related to certificate revocation is propagated by means of revocation lists, so called 'black lists'. Revocation lists must be made publicly available, for instance by being placed in a public directory.

The process of how the user actually gets certified and interacts with the CA may vary greatly depending on the application's needs. The two principle alternatives, which have different security implications, are:

- The CA generates the asymmetric key pair, certifies the public component, and provides the user the secret key, the certificate (which includes the public key) and possibly own certificates which link the whole thing to a common root key.
- The user generates the asymmetric key pair and sends the public component to the CA. The CA certifies this, and provides the user the certificate and possibly own certificates which link the whole thing to a common root key.

In the first case there is a need for confidentiality-protected information exchange, in the latter not. Confidential transmission from the CA to the user is easy if a smartcard is being used, which is generated at the CA site and physically delivered to the user. In case of transmission in an electronic form a symmetric encryption key (or a password where a key can be derived from) has to be transmitted out-of-band. In the first case, the certification authority has control over the quality of the generated keys, in the latter case the user has complete control over his private key. In both cases, however, an out-of-band information provision has to take place that gives the CA the required level of confidentiality in the user's identity and name to be certified.

The use of public key cryptography makes it necessary that one knows and trusts other's public keys. Public directories like X.500 directories may play a supporting role here. Users and CAs (if they are involved) have the following requirements when they use security services on the basis of public key cryptography:

- Users have the requirement to make their certificates publicly available and to have access to certificates of others and revocation lists in order to find out whether a certificate in question is still valid or has been revoked.
- Certification authorities have the requirement to make their certificates and revocation lists publicly available to a distributed community.
- Certification authorities have the requirement to exchange cross certificates with other

certification authorities and make them publicly available.

A public directory appears not only as information provider as part of the public security infrastructure, but also as user of security services in order to protect its stored information from unauthorized access and to protect its communication. Security policies in case of the globally distributed X.500 Directory must aim at three major goals:

- Protect the information base of the directory.
- Protect the internal and external communication of the directory.
- Protect the resources of the directory.

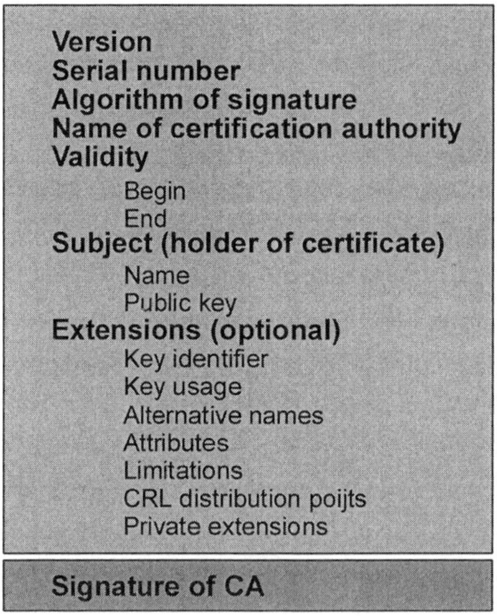

Figure 6. ToBeSigned X.509 Certificate

These needs were the motivation for the development of the **Authentication Framework X.509** as part of the X.500 directory standard where *strong authentication* methods on the basis of digital signatures and certified key-to-name bindings are being applied in order to protect the X.500 directory. The certification procedures and formats of X.509 are applicable in any context where public key cryptography is used. They are the basis of the "Public-Key Infrastructure of the Internet" (PKIX), which is currently under development in the IETF.

4. Security for E-Mail

In an email system, email messages are passed from one person to another via networks and/or modems over telephone lines. An email message consists of a header and a body; the header contains, among other things, the sender email address, the receiver email address and the date, while the body contains the message itself.

An email system consists of so-called Message User Agents (UAs) and Message Transfer Agents (MTAs). A user composes a message at his local UA which is then sent to the closest MTA. From there it is routed from one MTA to the next, depending on the destination address. Finally, if an MTA can connect to the receiver's UA, it delivers the email.

Today's email systems are based on RFC 821 [RFC821] and RFC 822 [RFC822] or the Simple Mail Transfer Protocol (SMTP); other systems based on X.400 have not proved successful due to their complexity. However, the RFC 822 format only supports simple text messages (with characters used in the English language), rather than supporting foreign character sets and multimedia types like voice and video. MIME (Multipurpose Internet Mail Extensions) defines the corresponding extensions, continuing the RFC 822 format, but adding structure to the message body and defining encoding rules for non-ASCII messages. By not deviating from RFC 822, MIME messages can be sent using the existing MTS.

Without some additional cryptographic means e-mail cannot be considered secure, because:

- We have no sender and receiver authentication. Although the sender and receiver are identified by their email addresses, those addresses can be spoofed quite easily.
- We have no guarantee of confidentiality and integrity. An eavesdropper will be able to read, modify or delete such files and therefore, corrupt its integrity.

An early solution for e-mail security was the Privacy Enhanced Mail standard (**PEM**) created by the IETF, in which public-key cryptography and certification à la X.509 where adopted for the protection of electronic mail. PEM's security mechanisms provide for confidentiality, authenticity, integrity, and non-repudiation of messages. Although PEM didn't make it's way into real life for a number of different reasons, principles developed there remain valid until today.

Another US development was **PGP** (Pretty Good Privacy), a public domain mail security program developed by Phil Zimmermann. PGP also applies a combination of asymmetric (RSA) and symmetric cryptography to achieve authenticity, privacy, integrity and non-repudiation, but uses a different approach from X.509 for the problem of the authenticity of the public key. PGP became very popular and is in wide use until today. PGP's current version supports numerous cryptographic algorithms for most common software platforms. Plug-ins are available for some mail-tools, like Microsoft Outlook/Exchange, Lotus-Notes and Eudora. Freeware versions of PGP are available for private use.

Currently, the IETF works on a standardisation of PGP, called OpenPGP, which supports the MIME standard for exchanging objects via email or other transport protocols. This standardization process is not completed yet.

S/MIME is the current e-mail security standard of the IETF, providing for confidentiality, authenticity, integrity, and non-repudiation of MIME-structured mail. Originally developed by RSA Laboratories, S/MIME

- adds authentication and privacy to messages in MIME format,
- provides digital envelops for encryption and digital signatures for MIME body parts,
- secures binary and text attachments,
- uses digital certificates in X.509v3 format,
- provides means for message wrapping or detached signatures,
- uses CMS (Cryptographic Message Syntax), a wrapping format derived from PKCS#7,
- is algorithm-independent.

Today, S/MIME version 2 is available in common e-mail tools, like Netscape Messenger and Microsoft Outlook/Exchange.

5. Security for the WWW

The most rapid growth of the Internet is coming from the use of the World Wide Web (WWW). No exploration of the deployment of security technology could be considered credible if it did not also examine the requirements of the WWW. In some ways WWW has been designed for complete openness rather than security. For example, there is no need for any log-in. Nevertheless, it has become clear that several forms of security are required, such as:

- The need to restrict access to specific WWW pages.
- The need to authenticate users who desire to make commercial transactions or access data on the WWW.
- The need to bind commercial terms from one source (e.g. a supplier) to a user - and

have the resulting transaction be confidential, all parties authenticated, and the resulting transaction be non-repudiable.

- The need to have non-repudiable content from the WWW available to clients.

The purpose of the Secure Sockets Layer (SSL) protocol is to provide secure communication between client and server applications on the Internet. SSL provides for message privacy, message integrity, and mutual authentication of the client/server system. It is layered between application protocols (such as WWW, FTP, email) and network protocols (such as TCP/IP, IPX/SPX).

SSL establishes a secure synchronous channel, where the security features are applied to protocol data units, so-called records, rather than to whole user documents. Once a secure channel is established between client and server, user data is fragmented into SSL records, compressed, cryptographically processed, and sent to the server application which reverses this process.

SSL secure channels are established and maintained employing five protocols:

- *SSL-Handshake-Protocol*
  An agreement on cryptographic parameters, such as cryptographic algorithms and keys, and authentication of server [and client]. The latter is done by exchanging server [and client] X.509 certificates.

- *SSL-ChangeCipherSpec-Protocol*
  Change of cryptographic parameters during SSL communication.

- *SSL-Alert-Protocol*
  Exchange of error and warning messages.

- *SSL-ApplicationData-Protocol*
  Transmission of user data.

- *SSL-Record-Protocol*
  Base protocol for all protocols mentioned above, responsible for fragmentation/defragmentation, compression/decompression, and cryptographic processing (encryption/decryption).

The original SSL protocol, SSL 2.0, was designed by Netscape and implemented at the end of 1994 in Netscape's Navigator and HTTP-Server. SSL 3.0 improved the original protocol, for example, by preventing specific security attacks and supporting more cryptographic algorithms.

SSL 3.0 is supported in all common WWW browsers and servers. In the meantime, the Internet Engineering Task Force (IETF) has standardised SSL; the resulting protocol, called Transaction Layer Security 1.0 (TLS 1.0), is generally accepted.

SSL does not provide any means for authenticity, integrity and non-repudiation of web contents. The Digital Signature Initiative of the World-Wide Web Consortium (W3C) created a standard for this, that so far has not gained much support. Also, an attempt of the IETF to add security mechanisms to the HTTP protocol, called S-HTTP, failed to win support in the industry and in the Internet community.

6. IP Security

At the network layer, the Internet Protocol (IP) provides for unreliable best-effort and connectionless delivery of datagrams. A datagram is routed through the network depending on the destination address. Multiple routers are usually involved throughout the journey.

Neither the current IP version, IPv4, nor IPv6 make any provision for securing IP packets cryptographically. The IP Security Protocol Working Group (IPSec) of the IETF developed at set of mechanisms to protect client protocols of IP.

7. IPsec

- facilitates direct IP connectivity between sensitive hosts through untrusted networks,
- prevents users from erecting barriers which impedes normal use of the Internet,
- provides application-independent security.

It is, however, no substitute for application layer security. The main features of IPSec are:

- It relies on cryptographic proof rather than easily forged IP addresses.
- It provides for interoperable router and end-system implementations.
- It enables for separation between authentication and confidentiality to allow wide deployment.

- It has algorithm-independent design, but standard default algorithms are specified.

- The key management protocol (IKE) is separate from the IP security protocol.

- It is suited for both IPv4 and IPv6.

IPsec proivides two cryptographic security mechanisms: *IP Authentication Header (AH)* and *IP Encapsulating Security Payload (ESP)*. The first provides integrity and authentication without confidentiality. This is done by means of digital signatures. The lack of confidentiality features means that this type of datagram can be widely available on the Internet, even in countries where the use of encryption to provide confidentiality is problematic. The second provides confidentiality and might also provide integrity and authentication. Integrity and authentication are achieved by means of digital signatures, whereas confidentiality is achieved using encryption techniques. AH and ESP may be used together or separately.

ESP can be used in two modes:

- The tunnel-mode encapsulates an entire IP datagram;
- The transport-mode encapsulates an upper-layer protocol (e.g. TCP or UDP) and prepends an IP header in clear.

This allows for various layering options and modes of application of IPSec, either in an end-to-end fashion between IP hosts, or in route-router or host-router configurations in order to tunnel through untrusted networks.

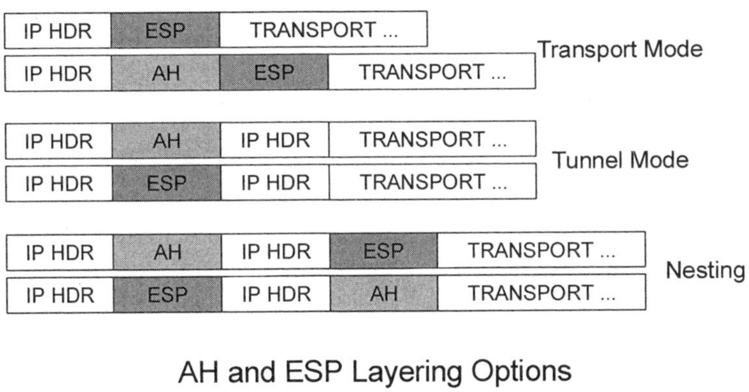

Figure 7. AH and ESP Layering Options

In IPsec, a *Security Association (SA)* between two IP stations determines how datagrams are cryptographically handled when being transmitted between them. A *Security Association* is a long-term agreement between any two IP stations (hosts and/or gateways) regarding the cryptographic parameters necessary to establish a secure connection. Parameters include the cryptographic algorithms for both AH and ESP, corresponding keys and their lifetime, and the overall lifetime of the Security Association. The combination of a given Security Parameter Index (SPI) and a destination address uniquely identifies a Security Association, that is, the receiving IP station can identify a Security Association by interpreting the value of SPI in an IP datagram.

Network Empowerment
O.B. Popov (Ed.)
IOS Press, 2004

David Billard

Charging and Accounting Technology for the Internet: the CATI Project

1. Introduction

Recent studies show that much of Electronic Commerce activities will be conducted via the Internet encompassing business-business, as well as client-business and administration-business relationships. However, the Internet has not been designed to support such activities and it lacks many features, as Quality of Service requirements or Charging and Accounting facilities.

At the beginning of 1998, the Swiss National Science Foundation (SNF) launched a priority program on Electronic Commerce. In the framework of this program, our contribution is the "Charging and Accounting Technology for the Internet - CATI" project.

The CATI project aims at providing a sound basis for the commerce of network services by Internet Service Provider (ISPs). The services considered are:

- connections with Quality of Service requirements (security, bandwidth, jitter, etc.);
- configuration and management services for closed Virtual Private Networks (VPN) where Quality of Service requirements have been specified;
- accounting and charging services in order to determine resource usage and to allow the integration of different pricing schemes;
- integrated and online payment for services; reservation-based services like ReSource ReserVation Protocol (Integrated Service-IntServ) for access networks to the Internet, and/or aggregated-based services (Diferentiated service-Diffserv) for the Internet backbone providers.

The CATI project is particularly relevant for the developing countries. The access to the Internet through low capacity links needs efficient distribution and sharing among the participants.

The paper contains the overall presentation of the CATI project and its goal is to introduce the architectural choices and proposals, we have made, in terms of accounting and charging.

2. Motivation and context

2.1 Context

This paper concerns the design and implementation of charging and accounting mechanisms based on available Internet Protocol (IP), which is a packet-based protocol. The current state of research and development in the area of charging and accounting of the Internet services and other networking technologies has been determined within the SNF- funded pre-study on "Customer Care, Accounting, Charging, Billing, and Pricing" [1]. This pre-study provides the most important reference section on international research activities and has been a catalyser for the CATI project.

The project discusses charging and accounting protocols and Virtual Private Network (VPN) services in the Internet. These services lack new mechanisms for collecting charging and accounting information such as the number of transmitted packets and the duration of the communication. This information will be used to determine the resource and service usage.

With respect to the charging and accounting work, appropriate protocol extensions for the ReSource reserVation Protocol (RSVP) have been defined in terms of new objects [2].

CATI maintains a reservation-based architecture for the access to the Internet and an aggregated-based architecture for Internet backbone providers. In addition, CATI proposes the integration of charging and accounting in IntServ [3] and DiffServ [4] as well as in IP-VPN.

Based on an Electronic Commerce application, a demonstrator is established including an IP telephony scenario, which implements the designed charging and accounting mechanisms. This demonstrator as a part of the second project on "Management, Evaluation, Demonstrator, and Business-MEBeD" that will show the efficiency of the CATI project.

2.2 Motivation

The Internet is known as an open and heterogeneous networking infrastructure. For E-Commerce ISPs, users and networking equipment have to be integrated. These new services and equipments need new management/control systems for charging and accounting information necessary to recover the cost of the communication[5]. Charging and accounting issues have never been solved before in the Internet for several reasons, particularly the public funding of Internet infrastructure and the presence of many non commercial services (Universities, public research laboratories). Some volume-based pricing schemes mostly used for the Internet (e.g., connectionless and packet-based network) in the past, were somewhat satisfactory and beneficial (to recover costs due to the network usage), but they have resulted in sub-optimal network usage.

Today, from a commercial and economic point of view there is a need for new mechanisms and control to allow a service provider to receive feedback about the usage of services and the recovery of the communication costs. These new needs are due to the combination of several factors. The most important are:

- the emergence of isolated and private users/companies and more commercial Internet users;
- the emergence of IP service classes, which require more fine-grained accounting and control: integrated services and differentiated services;
- the integration of novel protocols like resource reservation protocols and flow aggregation approaches;
- the integration of VPN technology with service brokers.

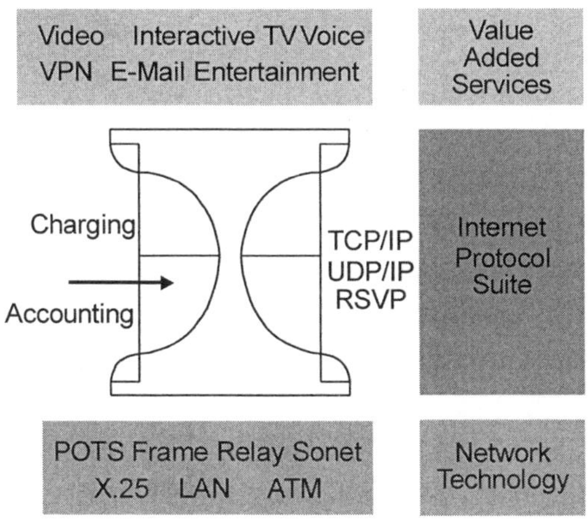

Figure 1: Hour-glass model for the Internet

Therefore the research focuses on the well-known hour-glass (Figure 1), which describes the relationship between network technology, Internet protocols, and value-added services.

Section 3 of the paper describes the overall CATI architecture, while section 4 discusses more in detail the different components of this architecture. Section 5 talks about the integration of Intserv and DiffServ within the CATI architecture. Section 6 underlines several pricing models discussed in CATI. Finally, in section 7 related work is summarized and preliminary conclusions are drawn.

3. General CATI architecture and CATI IP telephony scenario

To simplify, the IntServ over DiffServ architecture consists of two IntServ networks (stub networks) interconnected by a large DiffServ network (transit network) (Figure 2). The stub networks contains IntServ capable hosts and at least one edge router located at the boundary of the RSVP/IntServ network. This edge router owns one RSVP capable part which interacts with the IntServ network and one DiffServ capable part which interacts with a DiffServ control component to provide admission control feedback to the hosts generating RSVP signalling. The transit network passes several Internet Service Providers (ISPs) and can provide different Quality of Service (QoS) levels by applying per-hop-behaviors (PHBs). The transit network is not able to handle RSVP messages, but can carry them transparently. At its boundaries, *e.g*, ingress and egress points, the transit network owns the boundary routers. The boundary routers provide traffic conditioning functions to ensure that the traffic conforms to the Service Level Agreement (SLA) which is a contract negotiated between IntServ hosts and DiffServ ISP or between two DiffServ ISPs [2].

The CATI project also includes an architecture which deploys a Virtual Private Network (VPN) in combination with the DiffServ network. In fact, a VPN is open at the beginning of the transit network by the ingress router and closed at the end of the transit network by the egress router. Section 4 points out in a greater detail the motivation of the different architectural choices in CATI.

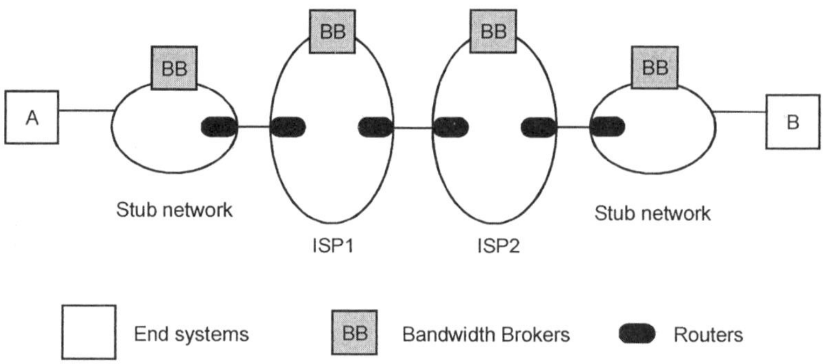

Figure 2: CATI architecture with bandwidth brokers

In the first step, an IP phone will be proposed as a stand-alone application making charging and accounting information directly available at the user interface. In the second step, this IP phone application will be integrated in a more general Electronic Commerce environment as a support of on-line communication during an E-Commerce transaction (on-line purchase, advertisement). Based on the previously described architecture, an IntServ customer A wants to contact another customer B (either a user or a E-Commerce site) through a VPN in order to run a secure business application. User A dials user B indicating as minimum his name, the desired QoS and eventually the cost-sharing of the current communication. User B could accept or reject the call. Before the communication, every user has a pre-configured user profile that contains default informations such as:

- sender identity;
- default IP provider;
- payment method;
- invoice/billing information;
- default QoS;
- default cost-sharing scheme.

All these parameters let the network retrieve information after accepting connection and initiating communication between user A and B. The information is used to charge the user for the current communication according to a pricing scheme.

While some default parameters can be changed dynamically during the call like the QoS and the cost-sharing scheme, others are almost fixed (like the payment information and the invoice/billing scheme).

This scenario requires several level of hierarchies at the user interface.

- *level 1:* the user chooses default policy for the usage of the phone and its configuration. The default configuration contains at least permanent parameters like the sender identity and the default IP provider and is saved in a configuration file. Each time, before a call, the user can change the information contained in the configuration file.
- *level 2:* the level contains a simple interface for calling purposes. In the ultimate case, the interface is reduced to the destination address and a submit/cancel button for the call. For an advanced user, this level can be enhanced by separate buttons specifying the more detailed parameters such as the QoS.
- *level 3:* during the call, the users may want to retrieve some financial data, through a feedback, such as the current price per unit for the call, the current balance or an eventual alert if he pays with a smart card. This user interface is on the screen during the call (it may disappear on a request by the user required or at the end of the call).
- *level 4:* after the call, the user can launch an interface for invoice/billing, aggregated charges which should be hidden in the level 1.

The Internet Telephony is an interesting scenario because it points out significant aspects of charging and accounting in the Internet: at the technical level, it poses the problem of an acceptable QoS for the two communicating parts, and the problem of better pricing schemes with usage-based charging. All this requires more fine-grained accounting information from the network.

4. Configuration and management architecture of the VPNs in CATI

VPNs consist only on setting up a logical and secure tunnel through the public Internet, which is intrinsically insecure. Therefore, VPNs use a variety of protocols (IPsec, PPTP, L2TP) proposed by the Internet Engineering Task Force (IETF) to ensure access control and privacy. However, a VPN could really become a bad solution if it is not properly managed. In particular, it requires an additional network equipment and competent administrators to ensure good connectivity and security. Moreover, an Internet VPN cannot in itself guarantee the Quality of Service. A VPN must pass through multiple Internet domains, which are mostly driven by companies such as Internet Service Providers (ISPs). The goal of these ISPs is to use new technologies and protocols (ATM, MPLS, RSVP, DiffServ) to offer QoS. These ISPs also have to collaborate with each other to maintain inter-domain services.

Therefore, CATI retains two basic components in an ISP domain: the Internal Service Broker (ISB) (an internal component) and the External Service Broker (ESB) to negotiate the service between adjacent ISPs.

The service can be handled in an orthogonal way or can be coordinated with other services. In the case of orthogonal service, a configuration daemon (CD) handles the local configuration of each machine of the network. The ISB manages a specific service local to its ISP via secure connections to the configuration daemons. For the collaboration between adjacent ISPs, the ESB can negotiate the necessary service with its peer ESB in the adjacent ISP domain. After inter-ESB negotiation, each ESB controls the local ISB corresponding to the negotiated service in order to trigger the adequate configuration.

In the case of co-ordinated service, a composite service server (CoSS) can offer a service combination. This CoSS can manage several ESBs and ISBs in the same ISP domain to combine several services.

When we have differentiated services, the bandwidth broker (BB) is an external service broker.

This entity automates the provision of the DiffServ between network domains. In the CATI model, this entity can also interact with one of its local ISB, and hence controls how the Diffserv traffic is sent through the network. This two-level hierarchy allows for a more scalable solution.

Concerning the charging and accounting between brokers, the previously mentioned ESBs negotiate the Service Level Agreements (SLA) between two different domains (either two adjacent ISPs or an ISP and its customer). These SLAs describe the volume of traffic that can be exchanged between the domains, the duration and the price that such traffic will cost. It describes how two adjacent ISPs or an ISP and its customer will be charged for the a specific service. In order to do so, the brokers use a signalling protocol that is in the focus of the current research [2].

5. Integration of integrated and differentiated services

Among several possible scenarios, CATI chooses an IntServ over Diffserv scenario for its signalling model.

CATI enhances reservation services with a charging interface to recover the accounting and pricing information at the application level. It uses a flow-based RSVP signalling protocol in order to exchange pricing and payment information. This results from the addition of new objects in the RSVP extension (Figure 3).

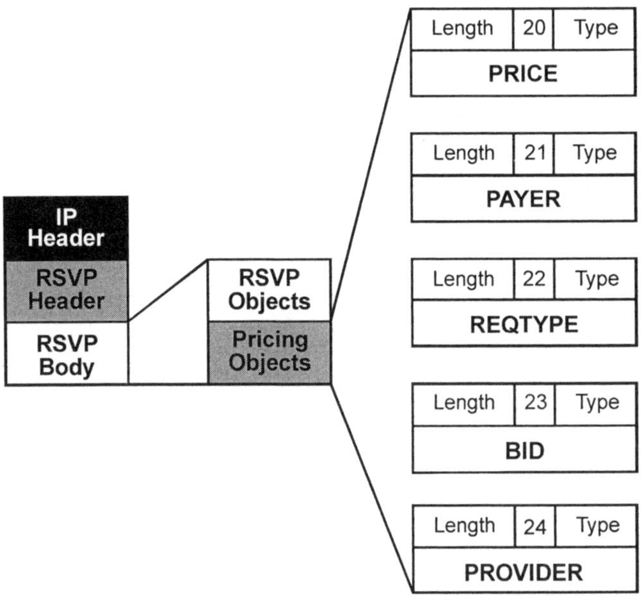

Figure 3: RSVP Object Extensions

That is the price object for the exchange of the market price between the sender and the receiver, the payer object for the exchange of the payer identity between the sender and the receiver (sender, receiver or both), the provider for the exchange of the provider identity and the bid object for the information of the highly dynamic pricing models.

In order to add QoS in a VPN solution, and to eliminate a real drawback compared to a leased line, CATI proposes differentiated services. DiffServ is a solution that matches perfectly VPN for several reasons:

- DiffServ and VPN both use the flow aggregation approach, which limits the funding for the operation of a public network. With DiffServ, the former TOS field is used to specify the forwarding manner of the packets (termed as the per-hop-behavior -PHB). There is a classification of these TOS fields into DSCP classes [3]. And each class gathers many different flows. The CATI project uses also DiffServ architecture in the transit networks that are VPN networks. The flows are aggregated at the ingress router of the first ISP network. This is the beginning of the VPN. These flows are split at the egress router of the last ISP network. This is the end of the VPN. Note that the previously mentioned signalling between the bandwidth brokers should reflect this flow aggregation, which minimizes the scaling problem due to the flow-based signalling.
- In the case of accounting and charging functionality, both DiffServ and VPN can admit it at the border routers and not at the intermediate routers. That is the intra-domain resource management can be gathered at this boundary routers. This is called a coarse-grained management.

The signalling used in the Intserv and Diffserv architectures must be mapped to each other. RSVP is the main component of the IntServ architecture which is used to request QoS levels such as Controlled-Load or Guaranteed Service for individual flows. The differentiated approach tries to provide two or more QoS levels without maintaining per-flow state at every router. There are at least two DiffServ classes already defined:

- *Assured Service:* assured service does not provide absolute bandwidth guarantee, but offers soft guarantee. It guarantees that traffic marked with high priority taggs will be transmitted with high probability.
- *Premium Service:* premium service is used for time critical applications, which

require explicit bandwidth and minimum delay guarantee.

The obvious mapping used in CATI is the following:

- Controlled Load - Assured
- Guaranteed - Premium

The Bandwidth Brokers negotiate the Service Level Agreements (SLA) between two different domains. These SLAs describe the volume of traffic that can be exchanged between the domains and the cost of such traffic. In the case of differentiated service, a maximum bit rate specified in the SLA between the host and ISP, expresses the traffic the host can "inject" in the network. The ISP schedules the DiffServ traffic separately from the rest of the traffic and also sets up SLAs with their adjacent networks.

6. Choice of the adequate pricing model for CATI

Several pricing models are considered, in CATI referring to other approaches, and especially to the Smart Market model and the Profile model.

The Smart Market model is based on the Vickrey Auction model[6]. This is an efficient structure to manage network congestion. A user sends packets to the network with the price he is willing to pay included in the packets header. This is the bid field. During a pricing interval, the network admit the incoming packets in descending order of the bids until a certain threshold. The user is not charged with the price corresponding to what he is willing to pay but he is charged with the minimum of the bid prices of all the packets admitted in the network during the same pricing interval. Thus, the user pays just the congestion cost, which is the so called-marginal cost. The marginal cost for transporting packets over the network is essentially zero as long as the network is not congested. Therefore, usage sensitive pricing schemes appear to be a good candidate for congestion control mechanisms. The objective is not to raise profit but to find a pricing scheme yielding the most efficient usage of existing resources [7], [8].

The Profile model focuses on how to predict the expected QoS (e.g. capacity) in an Internet best-effort network. In this case, the user can specify his expected parameters in a service profile. Then the network can treat the packet differently depending on the service with or without profile. Packets that obey the profile are tagged "in" whereas packets that do not obey the profile are tagged "out". A suitable dropping scheme, during congestion, drops preferentially packets tagged "out" at the boundary routers. This mechanism needs relevant profile metering in order to tag correctly the traffic. The profile metering has to be introduced at suitable points (especially boundaries) in the network. The dropping mechanism should be generally at the boundaries. Thus tagging and dropping mechanisms work in a de-coupled fashion yielding flexibility and scalability. In this model, the user is charged according to its profile, e.g, a user with better profile will be charged with higher price.

The Smart Market model poses the pricing problem regarding the network behavior. That is the network behavior (congestion or no congestion), is going to condition the user behavior. The Profile model poses the pricing issue more with respect to the user requirement. This is the user profile, which is going to condition the network behavior.

CATI objectives are also determined to combine these two behaviors and to define a pricing model with a good balance between the control of the user and the network behavior. Such model will gather the technical area (integration of new network services, network scalability), as well as the economic area (cost recovery of the network usage).

The more relevant model is not yet selected, but we are focusing our future discussions in this way.

7. Conclusion

CATI project has already achieved some intermediate results. The parameters are now well defined concerning the charging and accounting protocols for reservation-based methods. An Internet telephony scenario has been designed and will be the basis of the demos in the future. A new VPN concept have been evaluated as the QoS-support with VPN (DiffServ). In addition, payment systems including an electronic payment are currently being developed in the framework of CATI and MicPay project (covering the micro-payment aspects).

A description of a business model for service differentiation is under development. Finally, CATI may eventually support efficient and flexible systems for charging and accounting in the Internet with full integration of VPNs.

Acknowledgments: This work has been performed in the framework of the project Charging and Accounting Technology for the Internet - CATI (CAPIV 5003-054559/1 and MEDeB 5003-054560/1) which is funded by the Swiss National Science Foundation, SNF, Bern, Switzerland. The authors acknowledge contributions of their project colleagues from the following organizations: Computer Engineering and Networks Laboratory, ETH Zürich: G. Frankhauser, G. Joller, P. Reichl,

N. Weiler; IBM Research Laboratory, Zürich, Communication Systems: G. Dermler; Institute of Computer Science, Informations and Communications Management, University of Zürich: H. Kneer, C. Matt, U. Zurfluh: Institute of Computer Science and Applied Mathematics IAM, University of Bern: F. Baumgartner, M. Kasumi, I. Khalil; SWITCH, Zürich: S. Leinen.

References

[1] *G. Frankhauser, B. Stiller, B. Plattner, N. Weiler:*
Pre-Study on "Customer Care, Accounting, Charging, Billing and Pricing"; Computer Engineering and Networks Laboratory, TIK, ETH Zürich, Switzerland, Pre-Study performed for the Swiss National Science Foundation within the "Competence Network for Applied Research in Electronic Commerce", February 18, 1998.

[2] *G. Frankhauser, B. Stiller, B. Plattner:*
Reservation-Based Charging in an Integrated Services Network; 4th INFORMS Telecommunication Conference, Boca Raton, Florida, U.S.A, March 1998.

[3] *R. Braden, D. Clark, S. Shenker:*
Integrated Services in the Internet Architecture: An Overview, RFC 1633, June 1994.

[4] *S. Blake, D. Black, M. Carlson, E. Davies, Z. Wang, W. Weiss:*
An Architecture for Differentiated Services, RFC2475, December 1998.

[5] *G. Frankhauser, B. Stiller, B. Plattner:*
Arrow – A Flexible Architecture for an Accounting and Charging Infrastructure in the next Generation Internet; to appear in Netnomics, Baltzer, The Netherlands, Vol. 1, No. 2, March 1999.

[6] *L. W. Mcknight, J. P. Bailey:*
Internet Economics; The MIT Press, Cambridge, Massachusetts, U.S.A., 1997.

[7] *J. MacKie-Mason:*
A Smart Market for resource Reservation in Multiple Quality of Service Information Network; University of Michigan, September 1997.

[8] *A. Lazar, N. Semret:*
Auctions for Network Resource Sharing; CTR Tech. Report; Columbia University New York, February 1997.

[9] *Home page for the whole project:*
http://www.tik.ee.ethz.ch/~cati/

Network Empowerment
O.B. Popov (Ed.)
IOS Press, 2004

David Martland

Techniques for Efficient Distribution of Content

1. Introduction

This article is presented in several sections, and focuses on three broad areas. The first is web caching and associated techniques, and can be considered an up to date review of existing techniques, and current research in the area. The second is the delivery of content over global networks, and is appropriate for future multimedia systems, as well as other commonly used data formats. The third is the use of LANs together with appropriate servers to deliver content to a modest number (between 50 and 1000) end users. The final discussion addresses the integration of LANs with WANs for the delivery of content on an on-demand basis in a global context.

The subject areas under discussion are very large, and many workers are contributing to these fields. It is inevitable that some useful material will not be covered in this article, which nevertheless attempts to balance the material so as to give the reader a good overview of the state of the art.

1.1. Background

Much has been written about web caching and multicasting. Luotonen (1997) and Wessels (2001) have both written comprehensively on web caching, and Davison (2000) has produced a comprehensive bibliography on the subject.

This section gives a very brief introduction to some of the major concepts used in the remainder of the paper, and is set in the context of motivating methods for improved performance for distribution of data via networks, such as the Web.

Later sections, on architectures for data distribution will also exploit most of these concepts simultaneously, and multicasting in particular will have a strong role as an enabling tool, not only for improved performance of existing data distribution networks, but as a means of making feasible systems with new types of behaviour, which can be seen not just as improvements of today's systems, but as providing radically different experiences for users.

It is anticipated that in the future much of today's broadcast radio and TV output could be distributed via networked systems, and these networks will be based on integrated services exploiting fixed networks - based on very wide bandwidth links using optical fibre, broadcast networks - digital wireless broadcast networks, perhaps similar to the Eureka 147 systems now being deployed in Europe, satellite broadcast networks, and cellular radio networks. Services will not only be one to many, with distribution of media content from a few broadcasters to many subscribers, but will provide the possibility of feedback, and interaction. The technical infrastructure to provide this will evolve gradually.

There will also be the possibility of global distribution of media content - something which to date has only partially happened with the development of the web, but which will become a usable reality for many end users, not just a relatively few interested enthusiasts. Thus in the future, devices such as TVs and radios will connect directly to networked services, and be capable of receiving content from anywhere within global reach. The quality of experience which they will provide will exceed current systems, and will be vastly different from the existing web radio and TV services, which demonstrate global reach, but do not present any threat to existing systems because of quality limitations. Note that the connections to networked services may not require a physical connection, since parts of the integrated network system could be implemented using wireless technology.

1.2. Motivation

The use of the web as a means of communication has grown very rapidly over about a decade, from its first introduction using text based browsers, and now many browsers commonly deliver articles with enhanced graphics, and even animations, audio clips and video sequences using commonly available plug-ins. The user base is frequently divided into two categories - those who have access via high speed connections, usually based within an organisation, often a working environment, and those whose access is via slower connections - typically a 56 kbps modem, which often only allows data transfers at rates of 40 kbps, or sometimes lower data rates.

It is often suggested that providing high speed connections will solve most web problems, and indeed high speed connections frequently do provide end users with a better experience, but there are a significant number of problems which arise from factors other than the basic connection network. It is technically possible to make contact with a location in the USA from Europe - even on the West coast - within about 100 ms, and to have a reply back within a similar time, giving a round trip time of 200 ms. East coast locations can be contacted within about half this time. It should then be technically possible to transfer data from a distant location at high data rates - for example, it should be possible to transfer data at 10 Mbps, which would make direct connection to a TV site in the USA from Europe a possibility, and the quality of the received data, when viewed as a TV picture, should be high, assuming an appropriate compression format, such as MPEG-2 or MPEG-4 is used.

However "should be" is not the same as "is", and in practice the service obtained from networks does not normally achieve anything like this level of quality, though it may be possible for some privately funded networks. It is of course amazing that the web works at all, and most of us are grateful for having it, but the fact is that for many people the experience of using it can be quite a slow, and sometimes frustrating one. It often appears to take several seconds before any form of contact with remote servers is established, and then download of even relatively small files may take a long while. This applies even if the user is attached to a high speed connection, and investigation using network monitoring tools suggests that often it is not the underlying network which presents the problem, but a number of other factors. Most users are not aware of the mechanisms which are used to present web pages, nor of the many problems which can arise due to each individual mechanism: all they perceive is a slow system.

1.3. Web caching

Caching is one mechanism which can be used to speed up users access to the web, though it is not a "silver bullet", and although it can give measurable improvements, providing several benefits including cost reduction, typical improvements in operation are likely to be between 20-50% - not an order of magnitude or more, which many users would prefer.

Aspects of web data delivery which affect the latency time include DNS lookup, transferring requests and data across the underlying networks, contacting the remote server and setting up a connection, locating or generating the data at the remote server, locating any plug-in systems needed, rendering the received data at the user's computer.

Even rendering text at the receiver can take a significant amount of time, as HTML text needs to be converted into instructions for rendering. It is quite possible to find short examples of

HTML text which can take seconds to interpret and render, even on today's high speed computers, and for these the rendering time at the receiver could be longer than the data transmission time. It is too easy for us to forget that each HTML document must be parsed and converted by a compilation or interpretation process before anything is displayed on the screen. Not all files contain difficult HTML, and many can be processed quickly.

Similar considerations apply at the server end of the link. Even once connection has been established, the server has to determine which file or service is required. If a file is required, it must be found, then delivered - this probably does not take much time on a lightly loaded server, but many servers are not lightly loaded, and delays whilst the server processes the request can be considerable. Some requests are processed dynamically at the server - for example generating a file of records from a database, and these can be expected to take longer. In practice, many servers generally do more than simply copy files on to the network, and many users do not realise that often HTML files which are delivered are actually configured for the browser which they are using.

More will be said on performance aspects later, but performance limitations are one of the major reasons why many researchers have studied caching, and why systems administrators have installed caching systems, and national systems such as the JANET National Cache in the UK, and the NLANR caches in the USA, have come into being.

Other techniques which have been developed to solve network problems include mirroring and pre-fetching.

The benefits of Web caching can be considered as follows:

- Reduced
    - latency time for fetches, which can often be satisfied by the cache
    - bandwidth requirement across links between the system connected to the cache and external networks
    - costs following from the reduced bandwidth requirement
    - load on external networks
    - load on servers
- Increased throughput

It is often said that there is no such thing as a free lunch, and Web caching is no exception. There are some disadvantages:

- It is possible
    - to receive out of date files
    - to suffer from inconsistent data
- Complexity increases and additional software and hardware infrastructure is needed.

The performance gains which can be achieved by caching are relatively modest, but in most present day situations the costs of deployment and the additional complexity are offset against a reduction in communications costs. For some situations, such as where communications are limited or very expensive, which applies with some developing countries using expensive links with limited bandwidth, or using satellite communications to establish contact with remote areas, the benefits of using caching are often very significant.

1.4. Browser caches

Modern web browsers have cache systems associated directly with them, which are installed on the end user workstation or PC. These cache systems use main memory and disc storage on the workstation in order to cache files which are used by the browser. Many Web pages are composed nowadays of many small components, often GIF images, which are used as logos, buttons, and other graphical elements. If a web site uses such small components consistently, then there is no need for these to be repeatedly transmitted over the Web, and they should naturally end up in the browser cache. Besides such small file components, larger files also find their way into the browser cache. This can improve the performance for the user of the workstation, and should reduce the load on the local network, but will not make cached files available for other users. To allow sharing of files which are commonly fetched by a group of users, proxy cache servers are needed.

Some users use more than one web browser, and different users use different web browsers. Unfortunately browser caches are not generally compatible, so this can result in a single user creating multiple requests for the same file, if different browsers are used on each occasion.

Additionally, content negotiation between servers and browsers also takes place quite frequently, and this gives rise to a situation in which different versions of a requested file may be needed by different browsers, and this reduces the beneficial effects of sharing files in a commonly accessed cache.

1.5. Mirroring

Mirroring is a technique which was developed largely for FTP sites, and which provides a complete replication of the accessible file store at different locations. In its simplest form, the end user is expected to know where the nearest mirror site is, and to attach to that. The benefits of mirroring are clearly that users can select sites which offer lower access delays, or faster download times - these two are not always synonymous. Also, if one mirror site experiences problems, users can switch to another mirror site to access files. It is apparent that having multiple servers essentially serving out the same data reduces the load on each, and provides better performance.

Essentially, mirroring provides complete replication of files at all mirror sites, though a problem can arise if files are updated at the origin site. In this case some of the mirror sites may not update their files, and out of date versions will be supplied. This is one example of a general problem of data consistency. In order to reduce this problem to manageable levels, mirror sites are normally updated frequently, and it is convenient to do this using the network. A complete reload of all the files in a mirror site may be very demanding on the network, so it is more common to only update files which have changed.

One problem with this form of data distribution is that there can be a lot of network traffic generated as files are updated, and it is possible that some of these files will never be accessed. Systems administrators who decide to install mirror sites should consider carefully whether the traffic generated will cause problems. Another problem is obviously also that most mirror sites provide access not only within the organisation, but allow external users to impose an additional load across possibly valuable network links.

Updating mirror sites can be done automatically, and at appropriate times, so that network activity is optimised.

1.6. Pre-fetching

Pre-fetching is another technique which allows smoothing of bandwidth demand across networks. Files which are expected to be used are fetched ahead of time, and stored locally.

Clearly there are tradeoffs between network utilisation and storage, though nowadays storage is generally available at very low cost.

The costs of obtaining a data item depend on the data transfer cost and the cost of storing the data once fetched. With modern systems it is normal for even a one time data transfer cost to be greater than the cost of storing the data indefinitely, though this naturally depends on charge rates for transfer, and the equipment used for storage. Until recently it was certainly necessary to either provide backup storage, which would raise the storage costs, or to erase data from storage, as main disk storage filled up. The size of disk storage which can now be obtained cheaply is very considerable, and for most purposes storage capacity of modern systems is more than enough for the supported applications. Even if it does become necessary to delete data, data can be backed up very cheaply to media such as CD-ROM or DVD-ROM, providing that there is time to make the backups.

Note, however, that there are still some applications which are very intensive, and require very large transfers of data across data links, and have very large storage requirements. These might include video production for TV, or physics experiments carried out on particle accelerators. Such applications are relatively uncommon, and for most purposes appropriate storage systems will be available which can retain data for long periods at low cost, and it will generally be cheaper to retain data rather than to repeatedly request the data across a network.

This last statement must be considered slightly more carefully. Firstly, if data changes from time to time, it is reasonable to fetch copies of the new versions as they become available. Secondly, although the charging basis for data transfers may effectively be relatively high compared with storage costs, there may be no direct cost penalty for additional data transferred. Once an organisation has a contract with a communications provider, the additional cost for transferring the same data more than once across a network might be zero, so there is no clear cost incentive for organisations to avoid this. The benefits of lower latency for cached data should normally apply, which will tend to reduce load on the external networks.

The agreement between the organisation and the communications provider may be based on a number of conditions and assumptions. For example, the communications provider may only agree to provide an average bandwidth capacity over a given time period, and on condition that the organisation uses measures such as caches to reduce unnecessary traffic, and to smooth the flow. Contracts which guarantee bandwidth over extended periods with few attached conditions are likely to be considerably more expensive.

1.7. Reverse proxy caches

While generally caches are deployed close to the end user, this has the benefit of reducing traffic between the end user organisation and the external networks, costs, and latency time for the end user, and some reduction of load at the originating server. Heavily loaded servers can have major problems, and the communications links into such servers may also become heavily congested. If a server is known to have a predictable heavy load, the demand can be served by using multiple servers. One approach is to have a number of servers each delivering essentially the same data, though another approach is to partition the servers according to functionality. It is common to separate requests for personalised, or secure data from general requests. Sometimes partitioning is based on knowledge of the browser software client used (using content negotiation), and many large Web sites now use different servers to deliver content to different browsers, such as Netscape, Internet Explorer, Opera etc., which is almost certainly not the intention of the original designers of the Web. Whatever form of partitioning is used, there can still be significant problems with the network in the neighbourhood of the servers, which can affect not only traffic into and out of the servers, but also cross traffic in the near vicinity.

Reverse proxy caches are cache systems which are close to servers, often on the same site, and which take load off the main servers. Thus if requests for a web page arrive, these requests will be pulled through a reverse proxy cache, and this effectively creates an additional "virtual" server, thus taking load off the main servers.

One approach for incoming requests is to arbitrarily, or randomly, assign them to a reverse proxy server. This can pose problems for some transactions, particularly those which are part of a personalised transaction sequence. This is because the HTTP protocols are basically stateless, though objects such as cookies allow servers to handle conversations in which recording state is necessary. Such communications are nowadays an essential part of many commercial transactions, and if reverse proxy caches are used it is important to ensure that all components of any transaction sequence are handled by the same reverse proxy server.

The use of proxy caches improves load balancing at the server site, but does not necessarily improve localised network congestion in the vicinity of the server. There are a number of possible solutions to this problem for a server site with a known heavy load. Duplicate server systems can be created at dispersed geographical locations. The problem then arises as to how to route requests to appropriate server sites. One solution is to use modifications of DNS lookup, and this can often be applied on a national or regional basis. Thus users who request the same web site within different geographical regions will have their requests served from servers within those regions. The origin servers can still be treated as definitive, and reverse proxy servers deployed in each national or regional domain. The reverse proxy servers will collaborate with the origin servers to ensure that data is kept up to date and consistent between them, but this will be a relatively low administrative overhead, and the benefits of sharing the load between a multiplicity of server sites, and also having geographically dispersed servers, to reduce localised congestion can be obtained.

Another use of reverse proxy servers is to handle data from small Web sites, or sites which are attached to the network using low bandwidth links. A high performance proxy server with wide bandwidth connections to the Internet can be used to provide Web hosting services for small business which each maintain their own web server, but are unable to afford the costs of running high performance servers with wide bandwidth links. This approach means that the normal cache mechanisms for ensuring consistency can be used, and the administrative effort of uploading files to the server site, or performing other forms of maintenance on the hosting site, can be avoided. The publishing site administrators maintain their own site, but files are automatically loaded to the reverse proxy cache as they are needed. There can be some inconsistencies introduced by this approach, which will perhaps take slightly longer to settle down, but generally speaking the effect of these should be rather small.

Often it is known that some server sites will experience heavy loads, but sometimes a server site may experience very heavy unanticipated loads. This can happen if it contains information which is generally of limited interest, but some event can focus interest on this, and the site will rapidly become swamped with incoming requests. Some heavy loads may be anticipated, but relatively rare. Possible examples would include sites dealing with taxation before tax deadlines. During much of the year these would not be particularly popular, yet just before the tax deadline people might be more concerned and server loading could increase considerably. Sports events may also give rise to similar behaviour - a new, and possibly unexpected champion in a sports event could give rise to a considerable number of unanticipated requests. This type of activity is called a flash crowd, presents particular problems, and is discussed in the paper by Zhiang, Flloyd and Van Jacobson (1997).

1.8. Cooperating caches

If a single cache within an organisation is a good thing, why should the same principle not apply to other points in a network where large numbers of requests come together? This idea has been developed so that several countries now have national cache systems. Obvious points for cache deployment are at the gateways for handling traffic going into and out of a country. Using this notion, if a request arrives at such a gateway, a cache look up can be done to see if the request can be satisfied at the national cache level, and if so the request is not forwarded to the origin server, but handled by the national cache. The same principle can be applied at several different levels, such as at continental level, or regional level. Although this approach can improve overall efficiency, it is possible that the introduction of too many different caching levels can increase the latency time, and if too complex a system is deployed the efficiency gains can become marginal.

An essentially similar idea can also be used within organisations, so that there could be a company level cache, which feeds into several departmental level caches.

1.9. Multicasting

Multicasting is a method of broadcasting data to many users over a networked data distribution system. It differs from broadcasting in that only selected users receive the data, and it permits more efficient use of underlying networks, since data is not sent to locations where there are no receiving users. Participating members of a multicast group can send and receive data from each other, but first they must join a multicast group in order to receive data. When they no longer wish to send or receive data, they leave the multicast group.

A special case of multicasting is when there is a single source for data, so that there is a single transmitter and many receivers. Multicasting is discussed in more detail in section

2. Caching - techniques

This section deals with some practical techniques for current web caching systems.

2.1. Web proxy caches

A web proxy cache is a software/hardware system which is placed between the origin server and the end user's browser. Often a proxy-cache system is installed on an organisational LAN, behind a firewall. There are several purposes of a proxy-cache, but significant ones are to reduce the latency time for fetching data, to reduce the external bandwidth requirements, and also to reduce costs - since costs are often related to chosen bandwidth capacity.

2.2. External bandwidth and latency

The bandwidth for traffic between an organisation and the external network is often fixed, and the costs to the organisation are related to the capacity. If the demand is close to the capacity, the performance will be poor with large latency, while if the demand is low, the organisation may be paying significant sums for unused bandwidth.

Mathematically, it can be shown that with random arrival times the queuing delay rises without bound as each link or resource approaches 100% utilisation. Typically this looks like figure 1, in which for utilisation up to 50% of the resource, queuing delays (also queue sizes) remain fairly small and manageable, and then the queuing delay starts to rise until it begins to go "out of control" as the utilisation exceeds 80%. The actual details of the function may vary slightly depending on the queuing situation, but the overall behaviour is of this type.

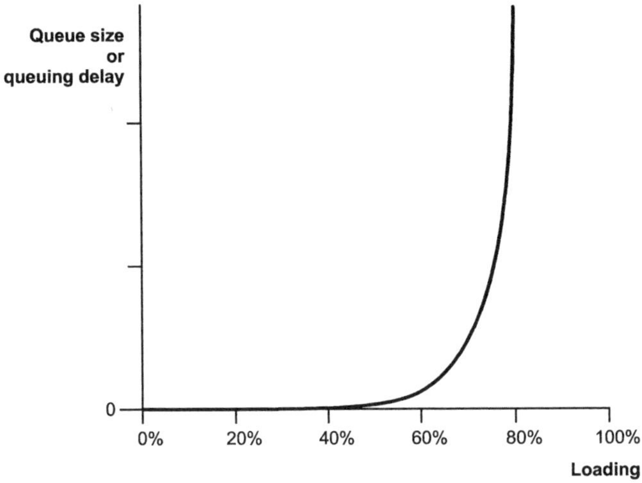

Figure 1: Queue sizes and queuing delays increase with loading

From curves like this, we can determine what an acceptable delay would be for a link, and then fix a maximum bandwidth utilisation across the link. Typically this could be between 50% up to 80%, though in this example 80% is tending to be unacceptable. In some situations even 30-40% loading can start to become significant.

It should also be clear that a reduction in loading can make a significant difference to the queuing delays. Using this curve, suppose we have a loading of 80% on the link, so the queuing delays would tend to be large. Reducing the loading to 70% makes a significant difference, while a reduction to 60% may give rise to a very acceptable modest queuing delay.

Suppose we install a cache before the network link. Each time an item is requested across the link, the cache is first examined to see if the data is available there. If it is, the data is supplied from the cache and not fetched across the link.

The **hit rate** for a cache is a measure of the likelihood of finding a file in the cache. Typically hit rate is given as a percentage, or a real number in the range 0 to 1. Thus if the average hit rate on a cache is 40% this implies that 40% of all file requests are served from the cache, while 60% require downloading from a remote server. A file which is found in the cache is said to be a cache **hit**, while if a file is not in the cache, this is said to be a cache **miss**.

Note that because of consistency checking, even files which are in the cache may require some communication with the server. The **byte hit rate** is a related measure, again measured as a percentage, or a real number in 0 to 1, which also takes into account the size of the files cached. Note that the byte hit rate and the hit rate do not have to be strongly correlated. Byte hit rate gives a better estimate of the bandwidth requirements. It is possible that a cache could have a hit rate of 40% and a byte hit rate of 30% - this would probably be because most of the files in the cache are relatively small. The converse situation is also possible if there are some very large files which are used moderately often. The bandwidth reduction due to the cache is calculated using the byte hit rate.

Let the byte hit rate on the cache be r (r is in [0,1]). Thus the loading on the link is reduced to 1-r on average. Apply this to the example, and let r=0.2, which is a realisable figure, and assume that the link is operating at 80% loading - which is almost certainly unacceptably high. The link loading is now reduced from 80% to (1-r) x 80%, so if r = 0.2 the link loading becomes, on average 64%, which gives a significantly improved latency.

For a bandwidth W, and a byte hit rate of r, the effective bandwidth is raised to W/(1-r).

If latency is satisfactory, then the effective throughput can be raised by a factor about 1/(1-r).

However, if delays are a problem, then it is probably better not to raise the throughput, but rather to benefit from the reduced latency time which should arise due to the non linear relationship between load on the network, and delay time. Because of this nonlinear relationship, even a relatively modest reduction in external network load can lead to a significant reduction in latency.

This analysis is of course still a simplification. It is assumed that the caching behaviour becomes essentially random with time, and it is possible that this is not going to happen in some situations. It could be that many small files are cached, in which case the link would be more heavily loaded when large files are requested. On the other hand, if the cache stores large files more effectively, then a request for a web site which contains many small files as components may cause a greater load on the link.

Broadly speaking the simple analysis shows the benefits of improved latency in general, but the improvements may differ in practice due to the nature of the data traffic.

2.3. HTTP queries and responses

In operation without a cache, requests for web pages are sent to a web server, and then the pages are sent back to the browser. The HTTP query sent to the server might look as in Figure 2 while immediately before each returned web page there is an HTTP response header, which appears similar to the one in figure 3.

```
GET / HTTP/1.0
Accept: */*
Host: www.ibm.com
Accept-Language: en-us
Accept-Encoding: gzip, deflate
User-Agent: Mozilla/4.0 (compatible; MSIE 5.0; Windows NT; DigExt)
Connection: Keep-Alive
```

Figure 2: A query sent using HTTP

```
HTTP/1.0 200 OK
Date: Mon, 14 Jan 2002 14:08:05 GMT
Server: IBM_HTTP_Server/1.3.12.2 Apache/1.3.12 (Unix)
Cache-Control: no-cache
Expires: Sun, 13 Jan 2002 14:08:05 GMT
Content-Type: text/html
Connection: close
```

Figure 3: A response header using HTTP

In this example, a page is requested from the site www.ibm.com, and the command used is GET. The returned response has a code of 200, which signifies that the transaction was satisfied OK. There are other response header lines, such as Cache-Control, Expires etc.

When a cache is used, requests for web pages are first sent to the cache. If the requested web pages are already in the cache (having been requested previously) it may be possible to use these immediately, in which case no request is passed on to the origin server. If the pages are not in the cache, then a request for the pages is passed to the origin server, and when the page is delivered a copy is stored in the cache, as well as forwarding the data to the end user client.

2.4. Data freshness

Practical cache systems introduce a number of refinements. Firstly, data may be in the cache, but may already be out of date. Data which is up to date is considered to be **fresh**, while other data is **stale**. Some mechanisms are needed for handling this situation, and the HTTP protocol has several. The Expires response header can be used to check against the current time. If the current time is before the expiry time, then there should be no need to fetch the page again from the origin server. However, although the Expires header should have clear uses, it is not always used, which presents a significant problem. Note that the example shown here has an Expires date which is earlier than the date and time when the page was requested. This could be used as an indication to a cache not to store the page.

2.5. Conditional GET commands

Earlier versions of the HTTP protocol used only a few commands for fetching data, but recent versions make use of conditional GET headers. A GET request becomes conditional if it includes one of several additional headers, including If-Modified-Since, If-Unmodified-Since, If-Match, If-None-Match, or If-Range. Figure 4 shows the use of the common If-Modified-Since form.

```
GET / HTTP/1.0
If-Modified-Since: Sun, 13 Jan 2002 14:08:05 GMT
Accept: */*
Host: www.ibm.com
Accept-Language: en-us
Accept-Encoding: gzip, deflate
User-Agent: Mozilla/4.0 (compatible; MSIE 5.0; Windows NT; DigExt)
Connection: Keep-Alive
```

Figure 4: A query using a conditional GET form

2.6. Validating page freshness

A request to a cache for a page can be validated by checking to see if the page has been modified since a known modification date. Using the If-Modified-Since conditional GET form, if the page has not been modified and page access is allowed, the header response code Not Modified 304 is returned. This indicates that the page can be delivered from the cache, and the cache can store for future use the additional information that the page was valid at the time of the request. Otherwise, since the round trip time for checking with the origin server may be considerable, the conditional GET will return a 200 OK code, followed by the requested page. This avoids the need for further interaction between the requesting client and the server.

A useful response header is the Last-Modified header, which can be used heuristically to determine whether cached data is to be treated as fresh or stale. In this approach, suppose that a request is made for a file on Mon, 14 Jan 2002 14:08:05 GMT, and that the Last-Modified field found in the cache is Sun, 13 Jan 2002 17:18:23 GMT. In this case the file was modified very recently, and it might be reasonable to assume that it could be updated regularly. On the other hand, if the Last-Modified field found is Fri, 30 Oct 1998 13:19:41 GMT the likelihood is that the page is not modified very often, and it might be reasonable to assume that the page has not been updated recently. A decision can be based on the date and time at which the page was last validated in the cache, and is often based on the ratio of the time since last validated access to the time difference between the last validated access and the last modification date.

There is a saving in latency time if files are treated as fresh, as there is no need to communicate with the server, and this saves round trip time. However, if based on a heuristic such as described here, there is the possibility that the file is actually stale. If users or system managers wish to avoid this possibility, then each page request must be validated with the server, which is likely to be very wasteful, with a large number of validation requests, an increased latency for retrieval, and lead to a large number of Not Modified 304 return codes.

2.7. DNS caching

If a file is requested from the web, it is normal to identify the IP address of the web host by means of a DNS look up. This DNS look up can be performed using either local or remote DNS servers, and typically gives rise to a short delay. Where the same files are requested repeatedly, this gives rise to additional DNS lookups which may be unnecessary.

A slight improvement in performance can be obtained by DNS caching, in which the IP addresses of previously located hosts are stored locally.

Sometimes, perhaps quite frequently, users make mistakes when typing URLs, and often they make the same mistake. A consequence of this is that DNS look ups are performed which returned no valid IP address. This form of DNS look up is the worst-case scenario, and will give rise to a significant delay. Thus improvements in DNS caching can be obtained by caching DNS misses, as well as DNS hits.

2.8. Cooperating caches

Within an organisation, it is quite reasonable for different departments, sections, divisions to have their own caches. This can happen for many reasons, some technical, some historical. For example, the legal and the finance department may share a cache, but the engineering and research department may have its own, and marketing yet another. One reason why this might happen could simply be that there was insufficient capacity in a single cache to supply the needs of all the departments, and another could be that the departments are located in different buildings. A consequence of this, is that different patterns of activity will build up in the different caches. Each cache will contain files which are particularly relevant to the users in the associated departments, but will probably also contain files relevant to all users. There will thus be some duplication of files in the various caches, which is wasteful both in terms of storage, and also in terms of the associated additional downloads. The IT department may decide to install a very large cache system which caches almost all the incoming files, before distributing them to individual departments.

One such configuration is shown in figure 5. In this configuration one cache (administered by the IT department) is the parent cache, while the other caches are children. The caches at the same level are considered to be siblings. Note that this configuration may reflect physical connectivity, but may be a purely logical structure. In this configuration, files may be stored at both parents and child caches. For example, a user attached to cache A may request a file. This will then be stored in the parent cache and also in cache A. A user connected to cache B may request the same file. This can now be fetched from the parent cache, and a copy may also be stored in cache B. At some future time, this file might be deleted from caches A and B, but still exist in the parent cache. Note that with this configuration duplicate copies of files in different caches can occur. This is not particularly desirable within an organisation, particularly if the storage can be used for other files.

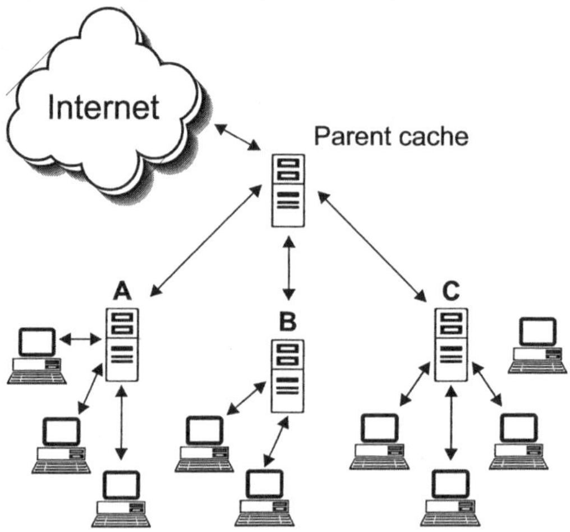

Figure 5: Logical structure of a caching hierarchy

However, it is also possible for a parent cache to be outside the organisation, for example provided by an ISP, in which case there can be benefits in having the multiple copies. If the caches can cooperate, for example by sharing information about which files they store, duplicate copies can be avoided, and files can be placed where they are most effective.

There are several protocols which can be used for coordinating the operation of cache systems, including Internet Caching Protocol (ICP, see RFCs 2186, 2187), Caching Array Routing Protocol (CARP), cache digests (used in Squid), and summary cache (Li Fan, Pei Cao, Almeida and Broder, 2000). Details of these are also discussed in RFC 3040.

The logical configuration of a hierarchical cache structure can be as in figure 5. However, if bandwidth on a LAN is sufficient, the physical layout could be as shown in figure 6. In practice it is more likely that the parent cache would be combined with, or closely linked to the gateway to the external network, but this is not absolutely necessary from a logical point of view, though such a configuration would probably deliver higher performance. This type of configuration can be useful when developing a network caching system, and for testing purposes. However, in high performance networks where the network bandwidth is in high demand it may be appropriate to use multi-homed cache systems, or for the cache hierarchy to be on a separate network. The details of a hierarchical implementation must be considered carefully by the systems administrators. It is also necessary to consider future demands, as opting for a simple solution early in deployment may lead to network problems later on.

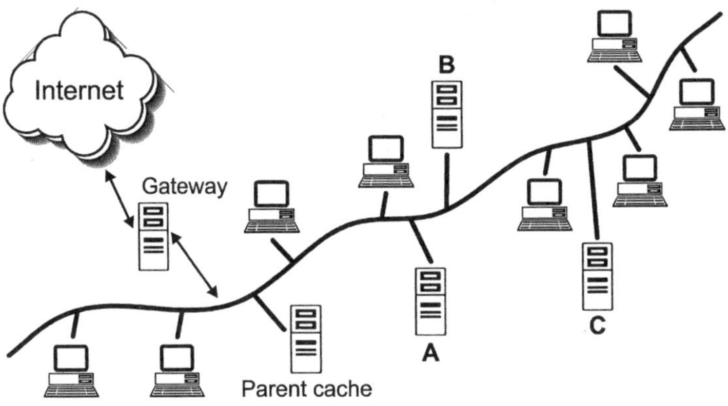

Figure 6: Possible physical layout of cache hierarchy

If each cache could be made aware of the contents of the others, then since all the caches are on a high-speed LAN, the caches could cooperate and only one copy of each downloaded file needs be kept. This would require that each cache maintains an index of all the cached files, and that the caches exchange information periodically in order to maintain up-to-date indices.

The operation of such a cache structure can be shown. Suppose a user attached to cache A requests a file. Firstly the cache consults its index. If the file is in cache A it is returned to the user. If the file is in none of the other caches it is fetched from the origin server, while if the file is in one of the sibling caches, a request is made to the appropriate sibling cache for the file which is returned to the user. In some protocols, cache A takes a copy of the file from the sibling cache, and then passes the file to the end user. Note that if the sibling caches are all on a fast LAN, it might be considered undesirable that a second copy of the file is stored in cache A, and in this case, since all caches are on the same LAN, the file could be returned directly from a sibling cache to the user. Another thing to note is that cache A might have an index which indicates that one or more siblings have the requested file, but this information can be out of date, so a cache miss can result. If all the siblings generate cache misses, the file must be requested from a parent cache higher up the cache hierarchy, or the origin server.

Protocols such as ICP and CARP can be used to coordinate this operation. In this situation CARP is effective because it avoids unnecessary duplication of files, and also avoids the need for large index files to be transferred between the caches. CARP works by hashing the file identifier using a hash function which is known to all the caches. This protocol emphasises logical location of files, rather than physical location.

For example, consider both figures 5 and 6. Suppose a user is connected to cache A (this may be a logical connection, rather than a physical one), but the other caches, B and C, are on the same high-speed LAN. The user requests a file which is not stored on any of the caches, so the file is obtained from the origin server, and its identifier is hashed in order to determine which cache it is to be placed upon. This can result in it being stored on cache C, rather than cache A. Subsequent requests for the same file at cache A will result in the hash function being applied again to the same identifier, and attempts to retrieve the file from cache C will be made. There can be a slight extra delay because of this process, but this is small compared with the delay incurred in fetching files from the origin server. If the same file is then requested from a user connected to B, this will use similar mechanisms to identify that the file can be searched for at cache C.

Cooperative caching requires the exchange of index files between caches, and if there are many caches this can become a significant load on the network. Summary cache ((Li Fan, Pei Cao, Almeida and Broder, 2000) and cache digests (Squid) are two methods can be used to reduce this problem.

3. Some advanced caching techniques and issues

This section deals with some more recently suggested techniques for improving web caching, and managing traffic.

3.1. Reverse proxy caches, networks, and adaptive caching

The discussion so far has concentrated on the behaviour of systems from the end user, and the systems administrator's view. However, there are other points of view to be considered.

For some web pages which may be in very high demand, a single server may not be capable of delivering the many copies of requested pages quickly enough. Further, a server in a single location may cause local congestion in the network. One way of reducing this problem is to deploy several additional servers. This can be used to overcome the server loading problem, but does not by itself avoid the network congestion. The additional servers can simply be mirrors, or can be proxy cache servers, in which case they are known as reverse proxy servers. If reverse proxy servers are located some distance away from the origin server, then the localised congestion at the origin server can be reduced considerably.

The deployment of reverse proxy servers is undoubtedly a useful way to solve significant problems, and is useful when resources are available, and when the size of the problem justifies it. However, it is quite possible that unanticipated hot spots can arise in a distributed network system, and in this case pre-configured proxy cache servers is unlikely to be a solution. For example, a news event may cause a sudden demand for information from sites which normally are only capable of handle a low rate of queries. This could give an immediate server overload, and associated congestion. Proposals have been made for adaptive web caching systems which adapt rapidly to this type of situation, using a network of web caches which can be allocated on demand to handle large flash crowds.

One mode of operation is to allow the origin server to handle loads up to some limit of activity, and then to start redirecting incoming requests to proxy cache servers which are allocated as the load continues to build up. Zhang, Floyd and Jacobson (1997) have proposed such a system, though large scale evaluation has apparently not yet been carried out.

3.2. Proxy cache server architecture

Luotonen (1997) discusses several different forms of cache server architecture. The simplest is to have one process per incoming request, but this is not capable of providing large scale throughput. Multithreaded architectures are able to provide greater throughput, and these can be extended to allow multiple processes, with each process supporting many threads. Starting a process, or even pawning a thread can be time consuming, so high performance servers often have many threads and processes waiting for incoming requests, rather than initiating processes or threads when requests arrive.

Cache servers can use a combination of disk and main memory for storage, and since both memory and disk storage are becoming progressively cheaper, there is little reason for not to deploy a high performance system with a fast cpu, and large memory with large disk storage. For reliability it might be appropriate to use hot swappable RAID disk storage. Despite this, useful small scale caches can be made using relatively small machines, which can nowadays be obtained cheaply, and for small scale applications a typical modern machine with 512 Mbytes of main memory, and 80 Gbytes of storage running a Unix or Linux variant, and using the very commonly available Squid proxy cache software, can provide good service. Large scale deployments of caching systems, such as the Janet cache service, typically use more powerful configurations, though the use of the Squid software running on Unix or Linux OS seems to be almost ubiquitous.

3.3. Cache replacement policies

Cache replacement policies can have an effect on performance, though the Squid software is normally configured to use LRU - Least Recently Used - replacement. This simply discards the file which has been unused for the longest period. Other strategies include Least Frequently Used - LFU - which requires counts to be maintained for each cached file, and Size, which uses file size criteria to determine which files to discard. Cao and Irani (1997) discuss a large number of different cache replacement policies, and develop a replacement policy called GreedyDual-Size which is claimed to outperform most existing replacement algorithms. They also discuss the possibility that replacement algorithms may optimise in a network friendly way, rather than simply optimising latency or bandwidth for the end users. Dilley (1999), and Dilley and Arlitt (1999) also review several different aspects of caching, including cache replacement policies.

3.4. Prefetching

Prefetching of data can be used to smooth out demand for bandwidth. Consider a pattern of activity as shown in Figure 7. This can represent the bandwidth demand across a link during the day, and in this example the loading rises steadily, with a peak at 5-6 pm. Also there is a dip around 5am, possibly due to system failure, but which could also be due to a very low demand. This information can be used to explain or plan the behaviour of the system. In this example, the demand on the system is high during the afternoon, and performance may be poor.

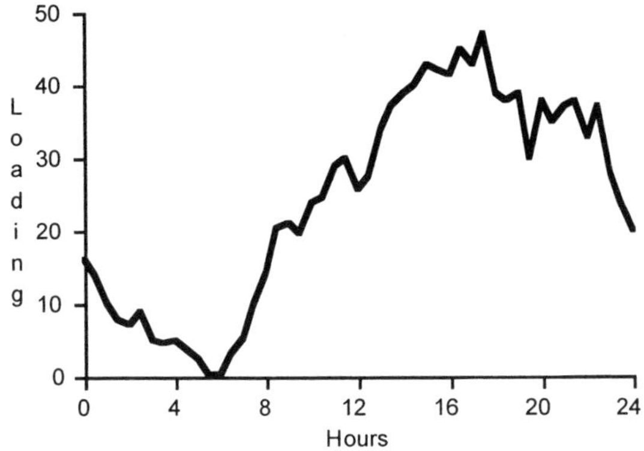

Figure 7: Hypothetical system loading over a 24 hour period

If some of the demand could be rescheduled to other times of the day, this could lead to a more smoothed out curve, and major problems could be avoided. Suppose that some part of the load shown in blue in figure 8, can be controlled and scheduled by the system manager - although this may only be approximately true - it nevertheless is worthwhile to investigate how this can be managed. For example, this load may represent automatic uploading or downloading of data to known remote sites, and a large part of this load might be schedulable.

The schedulable activity (shown at the bottom) contributes significantly to the total load when it is close to maximum. If this activity could be rescheduled at some other time, overall loading would be improved.

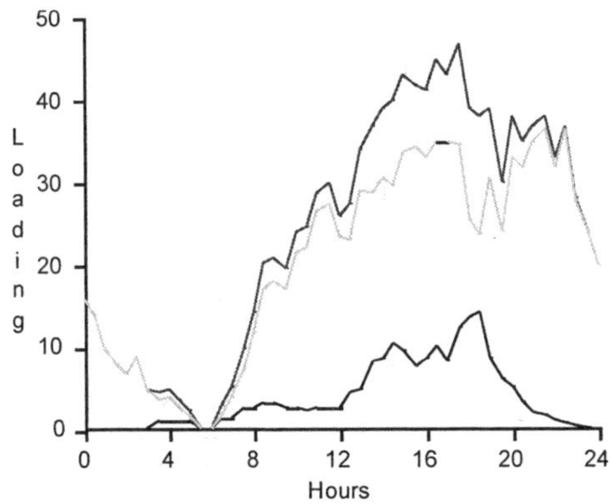

Figure 8: One task (the lowest curve) is mostly active during the afternoon. The gray curve (middle) is the difference between the total load and the schedulable task

This is shown in figure 9, which displaces the activity so that it occurs 7 hours earlier. It is assumed (unrealistically) that the whole activity pattern for this task can just be shifted to the left by 7 hours - with a wrap around to allow for 24 hour days.

In figure 9 the total load is now shown by the thick yellow curve, since the original load is reduced where the original scheduled task had its peak, and increased in region of its new peak. Notice that by this process, the maximum total load has been reduced slightly, and the general impression given between 11am and 8pm is that loading is significantly lower.

Load smoothing by organised rescheduling of traffic can reduce peak loads, and also reduce mean loads during periods of high activity. Even a modest improvement in bandwidth availability can have a beneficial effect on delays, because of the non linear relation between loading and delay.

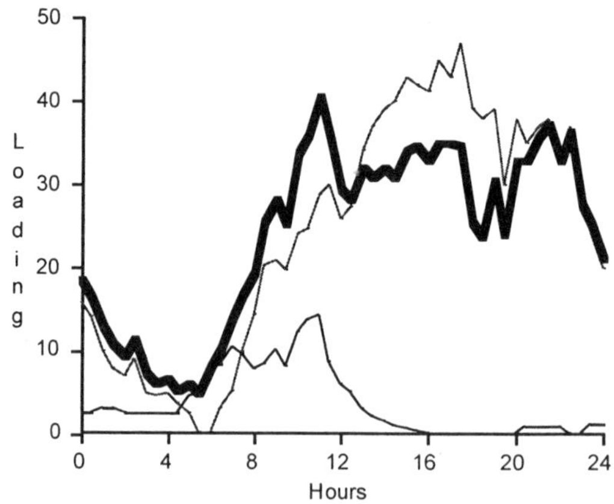

Figure 9: Modified load if the scheduled activity is shifted to an earlier time.
Here the scheduled activity is 7 hours earlier.
The total load is now shown by the broader curve.

It may be possible to reschedule the traffic to smooth out the overall demands, by predicting and managing certain types of traffic. This might be achieved by examination of data logs and manually deciding which traffic to reschedule.

3.4.1. Example

Suppose the work in an office is to write reports based on on-line newspaper articles. The newspaper articles are fetched on demand during the working day. Most reports are based on known sources, so it is possible to identify the sections of each newspaper easily.

Currently workers fetch the articles during the morning, as they require them. However, this is a time of high network demand, so downloading is slow. If the downloads can be carried out as the articles become available, this will both make the workers more productive, as the information will be ready for them later, and will also result in a more effective use of the network, as files are downloaded earlier, when network loading is less, and this reduces the load on the network later in the morning, giving better performance for other users.

In order to effect this pre-fetching, several solutions can be implemented. One is for one worker to come to work early, and download all the data, and store it for use by the others. Another is to have an automatic scheduling tool which fetches the required data, and again stores it for use by the others.

Clearly, if source data is updated during the day, data should still be fetched across the network, but a significant load could be taken off if most of the data is valid for at least 12 hours at a time.

3.4.2. Practical implementation

Pre-fetching for the news article example can be implemented as shown in figure 10. Suppose that the news articles become available early in the morning. Shortly afterwards, a program running on computer C fetches the articles required across the network. The data should obviously be stored on computer C, but a consequence of it having been fetched is that it should also now be in the cache, since the data was routed through it. When computers A and B subsequently try to access the same data, the proxy can supply it, though it may check back with the news source to make sure that the data is up to date.

Note that it may be necessary to ensure that all the browsers used for reading the articles are compatible, or that several versions of the articles are downloaded initially, to avoid problems with content negotiation.

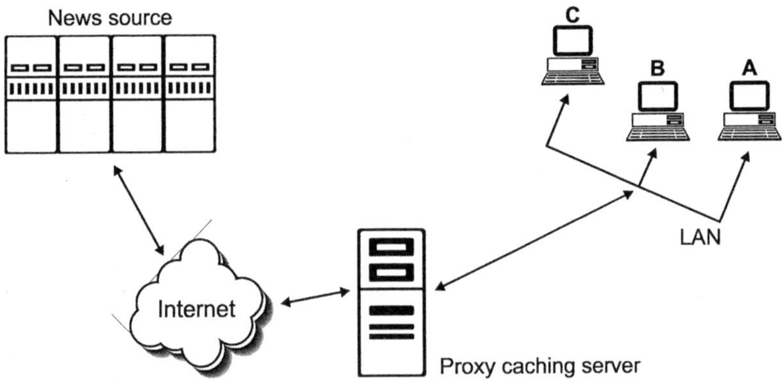

Figure 10: Use of pre-fetching to reduce network load - see text

3.5 Predictive pre-fetching

Pre-fetching and caching are similar in some ways, but differ in one very important way. With caching, data which has previously been fetched is stored, and reused if requested again. The efficiencies which arise from caching therefore come from users requesting pages at least once, where subsequent accesses to the same data are effectively carried out at much reduced cost.

However, users often request new information. They search for pages, and then want to find new articles with similar information to old ones, or possibly just even completely new articles. It can be beneficial to predicting which pages a user will access in advance. An "intelligent" agent could do prefetching. This might observe user behaviour, and then develop strategies for fetching pages in advance.

Doing such intelligent pre-fetching is rather hard. Each pre-fetched article incurs a cost for downloading and storage, but this is assumed to be smaller than for fetching an article on demand. Some such pre-fetched articles may never be used. The total cost over all the articles has to be offset against the savings for the articles which are actually used.

A brute force prefetching approach may lead to selfish solutions. Some users may be willing to use very greedy pre-fetch agents which continually look for possibly useful articles. This would result in reduced latency for those users, but at everyone elses' expense. Such approaches should be discouraged.

3.6. Top 10 sharing

Markatos and Chronaki (1998) point out that predicting what articles users are likely to want is a difficult task, but some methods for predicting for pre-fetching have been suggested which can be implemented by proxy cache systems.

They suggest cooperation between caches, so that each cache forwards details of its "top 10" favourite pages to other caches. In this context, the phrase "top 10" should really be replaced by "top N", where N is some number probably between 5 and 500, and dependent on several factors. N is actually not a globally set value, but is set for each cache. If N is set small, then only a small number of pre-fetches will take place. This may not be very useful. If N is very large, then a large number of pre-fetches may take place many of which will never be accessed, which is wasteful. Additionally, if N is large, the information which needs to be exchanged between caches becomes larger, and puts an extra load on the network. This method can be made to work positively, so that a significant number of cache hits can be achieved because of the top-10 prefetching, while the number of retrievals from origin servers which will never be used can be kept to an acceptably low level.

3.7. Possible improvement techniques

Methods for improving some difficulties with web caching have been suggested, though not necessarily deployed. One suggestion for both maintaining up to date pages at the proxy cache, and reducing the latency due to validation requests is for the cache to organise its files by origin server, and to maintain queues of validation requests. Then when there is a request for a page from that server, all of the files which potentially require validation from that server can be processed using the same connection. This method is called piggyback validation (Krishnamurthy and Wills, 1997).

Another interesting method for saving bandwidth treats the cases when files are modified, and a conditional GET will actually cause a new or updated file to be returned. Noting that often the modifications may be rather small, it is suggested that forms of difference coding are used, so that only the differences between the stored file and the cached file are transmitted, and that these are used to create a correctly updated file at the cache. This requires more processing at both the server and the cache, but it has been suggested that this can lead to a useful reduction in bandwidth usage. Typically the reduction in bandwidth is of the order of 10%, though this is quite a complicated algorithm, as different strategies for regenerating file copies at the caches will be required for different types of file.

4. Multicasting and content distribution

4.1. Multicasting

Multicasting performs a very similar function to radio broadcasting, but operates over data networks. These can be fixed, or wireless. Participants are organised into members of multicast groups, and group members can communicate between each other using a common channel. For the purposes of large volume data distribution, one group member could be the content provider, while other group members behave as receivers. The most general multicast behaviour allows more than one group member to act as a provider, and for interaction between group members. Here we shall focus on a relatively conventional one-many distribution process. It should be clear that with a one-many distribution, the transfer could be done by a source rooted tree - the content provider is at the root of a tree structure, and information flows from the provider to recipients. The distribution tree can be configured from normal network components - links and routers - and does not have to be fixed. With this form, users who want to receive from the provider must join the multicast group, and communications links to the multicast tree must be set up. Once a user has joined the multicast group, and the tree structure has been modified to send to that user, the user receives all the data that is sent out across the tree structure.

How the data is actually distributed can depend on the type of multicasting which is use. Multicasting can operate at the network/transport layer as in IP multicasting, and can also operate at the application layer of the OSI stack. Sending data out across the multicast tree can be quick, but this is not guaranteed, as it does depend on the form of multicast used. It should be clear that multicasting which uses parallel distribution will be much quicker than forms which use sequential distribution from each router.

Transmitting data reliably over multicast trees is more problematic than with one to one communications. In conventional one-one communication acknowledgements are used to indicate correct reception of packets, or implicit methods can be used in which packets are assumed to be correct unless a negative acknowledgement is sent. Since modern networks have low error rates, the probability that any packet has errors is low, and there should be only a limited number of acknowledgement packets needed in a reliable one-one protocol.

The situation changes with multicast distribution, as when the user population increases, it can be shown that even with low error rates, the probability that one receiver exeriences a packet error approaches 1.

With one-one transmission, in the event of a packet error, the packet is simply resent until it is received correctly, or the communication is abandoned. With multicast transmission, it would slow down transmission considerably if each time one receiver detected an error a packet had to be retransmitted across the multicast tree. Additionally, if all the errors are referred back to the origin transmitter, this can lead to what is often called server implosion. To produce truly reliable transmission, it is certainly necessary that packets are retransmitted, but they do not have to be sent from the origin server, but can be sent from any group member which received correct packets. Further, for some applications, such as multimedia applications, it is not absolutely necessary that all the packets are received correctly, since the applications can often interpolate data and tolerate moderate packet errors.

Bearing this in mind, several multicasting schemes first of all reduce the probability of packet errors using redundancy techniques, and secondly handle the retransmission of packets, if needed, by cooperation between group members.

4.2. Erasure codes

Redundancy techniques which can be used include error correction, and the use of erasure codes. Error correction allows correct data to be constructed even if there are packet errors, while erasure codes work on a block basis. An erasure code might work with a k out of n sheme, in which any k distinct blocks of data are needed in order to receive the data correctly. Such codes have been shown to be feasible for the transmission of packets in real time.

Using these techniques, multicasting can service a very large number of receiving users effectively, and the time taken to deliver a file of data to all the users may not be much greater than for a single user. Note that there can be problems with timing, depending on the networks used. If real time data is sent out, which requires playback and transmission to be in synchronisation, delays in the network can make this more difficult. To overcome this, buffering can be used, and for many applications a few seconds of buffering are not problematic. However, if dialogues are to be allowed between several users, buffering should be short to avoid problems.

Multicasting has a similar role to conventional radio broadcasting. This means that control of the schedules for transmission are determined by the sender, and this contrasts with the currently popular "fetch on demand" mode which users of web browsers have come to expect.

It is, however, easy to see that for commonly used data, multicasting is much more effective, and a more detailed analysis shows that for a large number of users it is at least one order of magnitude less demanding on networks than unicasting, and reduces the load on the origin server.

Multicasting is a technique which should work well for streaming data, and current Internet radio and TV stations could benefit from the use of multicasting distribution. At the present time the quality of programmes distributed via networks is generally limited by the bandwidth availability, which is generally insufficient for audio use, and significantly worse for video. However, the introduction of broadband (2Mbps- 10Mbps) connections at the "last mile" within developed countries, or the introduction of wireless technologies offering up to 11 Mbps, should make it possible to achieve high quality audio comparable to or superior to DAB, and moderate quality video. Future developments in network connectivity are likely to increase the bandwidth available within a few years, so that it should even be possible to distribute high quality TV over data networks. There may, however, be relatively little real incentive to do so, as digital radio broadcasting, and digital TV services will offer similar services, and not require connection to a network.

Nevertheless, the possibility of providing network based delivery would also allow the distribution of radio and TV programmes to take on a global perspective, and this might in the future represent a potential market which will be significant, and can be developed.

What could make both audio and TV delivery interesting via networks is the possibility of providing delivery on demand, when users want to access programme content, rather than when providers decide to transmit programmes. This is hard to achieve using conventional broadcasting methods, but if sufficient bandwidth and appropriate infrastructure is available, this can be achieved using a wide bandwidth network architectures, possibly with the cooperation of caches in the network. Such video or TV on demand services do not require multicasting, but they do place very high bandwidth demands on WANs if this is not used. A challenge, therefore, is to see if multicasting can be used to produce data on demand. This is application dependent, and has been discussed by Ammar, Almeroth, Clark and Fei (1998)

4.3. Data carousels

For applications such as software distribution, or large document distribution, or downloading of large files, a technique based on data carousels (Gemell, Schooler and Gray, 1997) can be used. Here the data to be sent is organised into a large number of blocks which can if necessary include redundantly encoded data, using error correction or erasure coding (Rizzo, 1997). If the blocks are numbered 1 to n, then blocks are simply transmitted in order 1, 2, 3 ... n, and then repeated 1, 2, 3... and so on.

Assuming that erasure coding is used, with k out of n coding, any receiver attached to the multicast tree simply has to receive k blocks correctly in order to download a file, or collection of files. There is no need ever to send any negative acknowledgments. Also, this method allows for receivers to work at different rates.

A possible problem is that normally the sender does not need to know how many active receivers there are, and some multicast protocols do not keep track of the receivers. As long as there are a small number of active receivers, the load on the network should be no worse than in any equivalent situation based on unicast distribution, and with a large number of active users should be considerably better. If there are no active receivers, the sender may not be aware of this, and keep sending. To avoid this, the sender should check to see if there are any active receivers or if the multicast receiver group is non-empty, and only send out data if this applies, though this should normally be handled by the multicast protocols.

4.4. Data Rates

For "computer" data, such as text files, the rate for transmission is often expected to be as fast as possible. Users usually want such files to be delivered with minimum delays. This can result in very high data rates being needed for large files.

It is now possible to keep multimedia data, such as audio or video data in large files, and to download these over networks for later playback. A one hour audio CD could contain 650 Mbytes of data, while a one hour video DVD could contain several gigabytes of date.

Note that optical fibres are now being deployed with considerable bandwidth capacity. It has been estimated that even a single optical fibre has a potential bandwidth of over 25 Tbps, and systems are now being deployed with bandwidths around 100 Gbps per fibre. Many of the DWDM optic fibre systems being developed and deployed divide the bandwidth of a fibre into channels with a bandwidth of 2.5 Gbps. At the maximum channel capacity of a 2.5 Gbps channel, a 5 Gbyte DVD (perhaps containing a 2 hour film) could be downloaded in 16 seconds - certainly less than a minute. This is considerably faster than real time data rates.

For streaming data, such as webcasts of live events, it is not possible to transmit at faster than real time data rates. For this type of data, the rate of transmission is linked approximately to the payback rate, although if buffering is allowed, the transmission rate can be varied slightly to allow for network delays and other factors.

Some users, connected by slow links, may be willing to have data sent at low rates, which can be lower than the real time rate.

4.5. Video and audio distribution

Distribution of video and audio data typically require quite high data rates, though some errors may be tolerated. For CD quality audio, data rates of 1.4 Mbps are needed, while other forms of compressed audio are effective at lower rates - 128 kbps is commonly used for digital audio broadcasting in Europe, though rates up to 384 kbps are possible, to give an acceptably high quality of received sound. Digital radio broadcasting uses MPEG level 2 encoding. In recent years MPEG level 3 coding has become popular for distributing audio files over the web, and this gives slightly better quality of sound for the same data rates, or can be used to compress the data even further for similar quality. Thus 64-96 kbps MP3 compressed audio is arguably comparable with 128 kbps MP level 2 encoded audio.

Video is also distributed using compressed video coding, and there are several different levels of quality possible. It is possible to transfer video satisfactorily at rates around 300 kbps, for video conferencing purposes, though the quality will not be perfect, the frame size will be small, and the frame rate will be low, and thus flicker effects will be apparent.

MPEG1 compressed video is optimised at around 1Mbps, while MPEG2 video is optimised at around 6 Mbps. High definition TV data will require more bandwidth, and also high quality master video used by TV stations also uses considerably more bandwidth. Professional TV studios use rates of 25 Mbps, 50 Mbps and higher, depending on the quality which they wish to achieve.

4.6. LAN based services

Modern LANs typically operate with 100 Mbps ethernet systems, though other protocols are used. Some newer LANS are running so called Gigabit Ethernet systems, with data rates up to 1 Gbps. Note that a 100 Mbps ethernet transmits at a data rate of 100 Mbps, but this does not mean that the throughput will be 100 Mbps, because of contention on the network and other problems. The practical throughput may only be 50% of the maximum data rate. Similar considerations apply to gigabit systems.

Nevertheless, it does appear that future LANS will have considerable bandwidth. It does seem that LANs with a practical througput of 500 Mbps will become commonplace in a few years. It is interesting to see how we can distribute multimedia across such a LAN.

If we assume that 500 Mbps will be a commonly available throughput on a LAN, we could perhaps allocate 400 Mbps to multimedia, with the remaining 100 Mbps allocated to "conventional" data communications.

DVD quality video might require data rates up to 12 Mbps.

MPEG2 video suitable for TV presentation works reasonably well at 6 Mbps

Uncompressed audio (CD quality) requires 1.44 Mbps

Compressed audio (DAB quality) requires between 128-384 kbps (Eureka 147)

Voice quality (telephone) requires 64 kbps (with dynamic compression using mu or A-law, but no other digital compression).

Compressed voice data may operate satisfactorily at 10 kbps, using compression such as GSM.

In Europe, it would thus be possible to service 30 TV channels using 180 Mbps.

10 Mbps should suffice for 80 radio channels (typically at 128 kbps).

Using methods such as bandwidth skimming (Eager, Vernon and Zahorjan, 2000) multimedia distribution can be logarithmic in the number of users, so that for 100 viewers, the network bandwidth requirement might only be 10 times that for 1 viewer (this is allowing some margin for operational reasons), so that it would require 60 Mbps to service 100 viewers all watching the same popular film on a LAN. Thus the three most popular current films could be serviced on a LAN using about 180 Mbps, to serve 300 viewers, giving a total of 390 Mbps. The remaining 10 Mbps could be used to support 150 telephone conversations (uncompressed).

This configuration should be sufficient at the current time for most European users, though users in the USA might find the restriction to only 30 broadcast TV channels, 80 digital radio channels, and 3 on-demand movie channels too restrictive. Such a LAN would be capable of supporting perhaps 1000 users simultaneously.

If high speed disk drives were attached at the server, it would also be possible to record all incoming broadcast TV streams for later use, though this would pose several problems.

Firstly, with an incoming data rate of around 180 Mbps, transferring this to disk in real time could present significant difficulties.

Secondly, the storage of over 23 Mbytes of data each second would require massive storage, and even if only prime time TV were stored this would require (say) 6 hours viewing per day, and a storage requirement of nearly 500 Gbytes.

This could probably be achieved with a few modern disk drives, though it is doubtful whether a few such drives could cope with the high data rates required. A specialised system, such as a RAID system, which spreads the data access over many disk drives would probably be necessary. A week's programming could be stored using approximately 3.5 Tbytes, which should be feasible, and possibly economic given the prospective number of users.

Thirdly, if local users were then to access the stored material in an on-demand manner, each user (assumed independent) would then require a 6 Mbps link to the server. This would clearly only be possible with 400 Mbps available if the number of users is restricted to about 60.

Fourthly, management systems for the stored programmes would be necessary, for example to delete programmes after a week's storage, or to compress them into less demanding formats if there were still sufficient interest. Logging user activity would be necessary to determine whether stored programmes should be scheduled for deletion, or compression.

Storage management would not be too demanding a processing task, but compressing stored data across a large number of channels could be, and it might be necessary to farm this activity out to other processors. It would be important not to transfer any data for this purpose across the distribution network, as this would reduce its effective capacity, though it might not be unreasonable to use a secondary network for such processing. It is assumed that in the early stages of deployment such LAN based servers will not cache incoming multimedia streams., thus deferring these problems.

4.7. Combined LAN/WAN services

The LAN based system proposed in section 4.6 could be combined with external services provided from a WAN feeder network. This would allow end users to have access to a wide range of services, including near video on demand (NVOD) services delivered over a WAN using multicasting.

Apart from providing end users with a much richer range of services, this method should also take a considerable load off the WAN content distribution. Popular content could be stored on the LAN based server, and this might then allow much greater control over the delivery, with end users able to utilise a large repertoire of commands, including fast forward and reverse, slow and still frames, and to bookmark sequences. Further, control would probably be much faster since there would be no need to send control requests back over the WAN, and indeed LAN based servers could operate cooperatively with client based caches to minimise the time required for carrying out any action.

This approach is already being adopted to some extent in the USA (Brewer, 2001), both for web and TV content. It has particular advantages for broadcast content distribution in the USA, where most stations earn revenue by advertising, as it becomes possible to target particular neighbourhoods for "ad insertion" - different localities have different commercials in the breaks between programmes. This could be less popular in many European countries where there is a stronger tradition of public broadcasting without a requirement to satisfy the "needs" of sponsors and advertisers.

There are also moves towards using such architectures for web content distribution, which has led to developments by commercial enterprises such as Cisco, Akamai and Inktomi.

Performance of some features of the combined WAN/LAN services may be restricted compared to LAN based services, but it will be possible to exploit the global nature across both national and continental boundaries.

5. Conclusion

This paper provides a brief introduction to some of the major aspects of today's networking environment, with particular reference to web caching and multicasting. Mechanisms for web caching have been discussed, and the benefits have shown typically to be a measurable improvement in some aspects, for example, latency, of between 20-60% in typical cases.

Multicasting has also been shown to have significant advantages for certain types of data distribution, with typically 10 times efficiency improvements for network distribution with a large end user population. Multicasting should also take a significant load off servers.

The problem of combining multicasting with caching in order to provide on demand services is also discussed, and it is shown that by moving appropriate functionality to intermediate servers that this can be achieved.

New architectural models are also proposed for content distribution across WAN and LAN networks which will be capable of providing significantly enhanced services for end users in the next decade, while at the same time reducing the need for the transmission of duplicate and redundant data across WANs.

The enhanced services envisaged will include media on demand, and will also have the potential for global reach. There will, almost inevitably, be problems with copyright and other issues relating to content distribution, but these are outside the scope of this paper.

It is anticipated that such services will arise inevitably, despite possible opposition from a number of organisations with vested interests, due to the reducing costs for development and deployment, and that during the next decade user expectations will rise rapidly so that architectures and methods discussed and proposed here will not only be of interest in research labs, but will become essential parts of future information distribution infrastructure.

References

[1] Ammar, M.H, Almeroth, K.C, Clark, R.J and Fei, Z.(1998), Multicast delivery of web pages or how to make web servers pushy, in Proceedings of the Workshop on Internet Server Performance, Madison, Wisconsin, June 1998.

[2] Brewer, E (2000), "Keynote address: Enabling next generation streaming media networks", in Proc. of ACM Multimedia 2000, Los Angeles, October 2000.

[3] Cao, P and Irani (1997) S, Cost-aware WWW proxy caching algorithms, Proc. USENIX symposium on Internet Technologies and Systems, Monterey, CA.

[4] CARP (2001), "Cache Array Routing Protocol and Proxy Server 2.0", best obtained by searching for "CARP" at http:// www.microsoft.com/

[5] Davison, B (2000), "Brian Davison's Web caching bibliography", http://citeseer.nj.nec.com/281347.html or by searching for "Davison cache" at http://citeseer.nj.nec.com/

[6] Dilley, J (1999), The Effect of Consistency on Cache Response Time, Hewlett-Packard Technical Report HPL-1999-107, Palo Alto, CA Retrieved on 11/1/02: http://www.hpl.hp.com/techreports/1999/HPL-1999-107.html.

[7] Dilley, J, Arlitt, M(1999), Improving proxy cache performance - analyzing three cache replacement policies, Hewlett-Packard Technical Report HPL-1999-142, Palo Alto, CA, 1999.

[8] Eager, J, Vernon, M and Zahorjan, J (2000), "Bandwidth skimming: a technique for cost-effective video-on-demand", in Proc Multimedia Computing and Networking 2000, San Jose, CA.

[9] Gemmell, J., Schooler,E, and Gray,J (1999), "Fcast multicast file distribution: 'tune in, download, and drop out'," in Proc. of the IASTED International Conf. on Internet Multimedia Systems and Applications (IMSA '99)}, Nassau, Bahamas, October 1999.

[10] Kleinrock, L (1975), "Queuing systems. Vol 1", John Wiley, New York.

[11] Krishnamurthy, B and Wills (1997), C.E, "Study of piggyback cache validation for proxy caches in the World Wide Web", Proc. of the USENIX symposium on Internet technologies and systems, Monterey, CA.

[12] Kurose, J.F. and Ross, K.W (2001), "Computer Networking: a top down approach featuring the Internet", Addison Wesley.

[13] Li Fan, Pei Cao, Almeida J, Broder, A.Z (2000), "Summary cache: a scalable wide-area Web cache sharing protocol," IEEE/ACM Trans. on Networking, Vol 8, no 3, pp 281-293.

[14] Luotonen A (1997), Web Proxy Servers, Prentice Hall.

[15] Markatos, E.P. and Chronaki, C.E (1998), "A top 10-approach to prefetching on the Web", in Proceedings of the INET 98 Conference, 1998
[16] RFC 2186, Internet Cache Protocol (ICP), version 2.
[17] RFC 2187, Application of Internet Cache Protocol (ICP), version 2.
[18] RFC 3040, Internet Web Replication and Caching Taxonomy.
[19] SQUID, Web pages on SQUID at http://www.squid-cache.org/
[20] Zhang, L, Floyd, S and Van Jacobson(1997), "Adaptive Web Caching", in Proceedings of the NLANR Web Cache Workshop, Boulder, CO, June 1997.

Network Empowerment
O.B. Popov (Ed.)
IOS Press, 2004

Ole Jacobsen

Towards Ubiquitous Internet Access

1. Introduction

The last 100 years have seen numerous technological innovations that have each had a dramatic impact on society. Imagine a world without electricity, railroads, air travel, telephone, radio, and television, and you begin to appreciate the effect that each of these inventions has had.

The Internet has been described by some as "The Second Industrial Revolution," and whether you choose to use those terms or not, the impact of the Internet on the developed world is readily apparent. This article looks at the current state and future prospects for Internet access.

2. Background

Throughout the history of technological innovation the world has seen many "unintended consequences." When radio was being introduced in the 1920s, it was portrayed as an entertainment box. Twenty years later, when the Nazi Army invaded Norway, they confiscated every radio set in the country. Radio had become an important tool for information (or propaganda). When computers were first developed, they filled entire buildings, and their designers estimated that the world would need only a dozen or so such installations. Today most people own (or have access to) at least one personal computer, and we are surrounded by computers in everything from our cars to kitchen appliances. All of this has been made possible by the invention of the transistor in 1948 and the subsequent miniaturization and mass production of electronics.

The Internet started its life as a US Government-funded network that linked universities and research institutions. For many years, the users of this network of networks spent most of their time on three major applications: e-mail, file transfer, and remote login from one computer to another somewhere else on the network. The introduction of the World Wide Web in 1993 changed this dramatically. The Web, developed by researchers at CERN in Switzerland, was originally designed as a mechanism for easy document retrieval by researchers - a sort of electronic linked library if you will. It soon became apparent that the system could be used not only for text, but also for images and other multimedia effects. Most importantly, the Web quickly developed into an *interactive* system. Users can fill in forms and have information processed on the fly by remote systems. This allows the Web to be used for e-commerce and other kinds of two-way transactions, including access to live information such as flight arrivals, stock quotes, and weather maps.

The shift that took place with the introduction of the Web made the Internet a household name. Today you'll find Web addresses ("URLs," or Universal Resource Locators) on everything from breakfast cereal boxes to city buses. It is assumed that "everyone" has easy access to the Internet, even though statistics about PC ownership and usage tell a slightly different story.

3. Internet Access

Statistics aside, the Internet has become an important tool for both business and personal use. Electronic mail has not replaced traditional business letters or faxes, but an increasing amount of communication is taking place via the Net. Most companies have a Web site, and most companies allow its customers to communicate with them via e-mail. The amount of e-mail flowing *inside* most corporations is quite staggering and has undoubtedly changed the way communication takes place in business. As a consequence, most traveling professionals carry with them a laptop, which they dutifully connect to the telephone in their hotel room to "download e-mail." This daily ritual is not without problems, however. In addition to the 26 different kinds of telephone connectors in use in the world, the traveler must cope with a variety of methods for dialing, metering pulses, as well as the intricacies of local Internet Service Providers (ISPs). Since most business professionals don't carry with them a traditional telephone set or a fax machine, it is reasonable to ask why they need to carry a computer, albeit a portable one.

Clearly, the technology needed to provide Internet access "everywhere" is readily available. What is needed is a reasonable business plan and some innovative thinking. One could, for example, imagine a smart-card-based system. The hotel room would have a combination TV set and Internet-enabled computer with a smart-card reader. Users would insert the card, the "desktop" of their "home" system would appear, and they could work exactly the same way as if they were sitting in front of their home or office machine. We are not aware that any such system is available today, but many hotels in the US have started to provide high-speed Internet access for a fixed daily fee, so the importance of Internet access for the traveler is understood.

Alternative lightweight solutions also exist. Hand-held computers (PDAs), and cellphones can now provide wireless Internet access, but screen size and input methods make such systems much more cumbersome to use. For short-duration "lookup" transactions, small devices *can* be very effective.

In parts of the world, the "home" or "consumer" Internet user is being offered high-speed alternatives to the standard dialup modem. Digital Subscriber Lines (DSLs) and cable TV modems can provide "always-on" solutions at orders of magnitude higher speeds than traditional telephone modems. This is a Good Thing, but only a first steps towards a fully Internet-enabled society.

4. Personal Observations

Easy access to the Internet for "the masses" is not merely a matter of providing enough low-cost computers and ISP solutions. We believe the following areas need to be radically improved before the "Internet Access Device" becomes as robust and commonplace as the telephone:

- Stable operating systems that are user friendly. In other words: better software.
- Improved browsers and user interfaces. Surfing the Web can be a very frustrating experience. Not only is it difficult to find what you are looking for, but often you find yourself in a "URL Trap," where clicking "Back" just takes you to the same page over and over again. The URL scheme itself isn't exactly user friendly either.
- Provision of Internet access in public places, similar to the way you find pay telephones in most parts of the world. The details of how such Internet terminals would be operated (and paid for) are outside the scope of this article.

5. Innovation is the Key

A couple of years ago, Sony introduced a new shortwave radio with an interesting twist. In addition to the usual set of controls, this radio features "Station Direct" buttons labeled "DW," "BBC," "VOA," and "OTH." The radio also features a world clock. By selecting the timezone that corresponds to the place you are and pushing, for example, the "BBC" button, the radio will scan only those frequencies in use *at that time for that timezone*. The resulting "database" of some 3,000 frequencies is held in a chip that can be replaced on a annual basis as the broadcasters alter the transmission frequencies. What is clever about this solution is the combination of three different technologies: a world clock, a list of frequencies, and a tuner. While shortwave tuning is a pretty specialized hobby, it does not take too much imagination to see how this concept could be expanded. Suppose we increase the number of frequencies in the database to 3,000,000 instead of 3,000 - not a difficult task with today's memory technology. This database could probably hold almost every brodcast station in the world, shortwave or otherwise. Imagine tapping in the name of a city and being presented with a menu of available radio stations for that location.

We believe that a future Internet access device will combine numerous technologies in a "clever" way, similar to the Sony radio. It will provide all of the features we expect from our most powerful computers today, at a fraction of the cost, and through much improved user interfaces. Accessing the Internet should become as intuitive as using the telephone, but this will require considerable innovation and "thinking outside the box."

Network Empowerment
O.B. Popov (Ed.)
IOS Press, 2004

Rolf Dalin and Karin Ekberg

Taking Distance Education to the Extreme: the CEENet Precourse & Workshop Case

1. Introduction

What could be more extreme in distance education than to launch a course entirely online to participants in more than twenty different countries? Well, maybe the other extreme: meeting many of those people face-to-face at the same place at the same time for an intensive one-week workshop.

This paper is about our experiences from an educational project, the aim of which was to combine an existing annual face-to-face workshop with an on-line preparatory course. The target area was Central and Eastern Europe: from Estonia in the north, Slovenia in the west, Macedonia in the south to Mongolia in the east. The workshop itself had as its main objective to train trainers in creating online courses in their various fields of expertise.

In the paper we will also outline from current theories of learning and of communications some basic fundaments upon which the outcome of this kind of distributed courses rests. It is far from enough to supply the technical prerequisites needed. Social, pedagogical, and managerial aspects also have to be considered (Berge 1995). These aspects on the learning environment and process need to be considered together with the technical aspects, especially when it comes to facilitation of communication and collaboration in the online educational/training setting.

2. Background

The Central and Eastern European Network Association, CEENet, was established in 1994 with the objective to co-ordinate international aspects primarily of academic and research networking in the region of Central and Eastern Europe. Organizing annual workshops about the Internet technology and services is one important way of achieving the objective. To this end two tracks, one on the Internet technology/hardware and one on the Internet services/ software, were formed in 1995 and in 1998 a third track on the pedagogy of distance education using the Internet was added. The purpose of the distance education track is to train trainers in designing courses including methods for distance education.

The 1998 workshop was the first for the educational track. It was conducted with traditional face-to-face sessions for eight days in Bratislava, Slovakia. The workshop contained lectures on topics like learning theories, target group analysis, case studies of experiences from Internet supported DE, content analysis, objectives and assessment, instructional strategies, telecommunication, online collaboration and design of learning environments. Practical project work was also on the agenda, but was not given more than approximately 10-20 % of the workshop working hours. For these project sessions the participants had access to a web-based comprehensive course environment called WebCT (Web Course Tool, **www.about.webct.com**). This environment was used for practising web-based course design.

In Bratislava 1998 possible future developments for the educational workshops were discussed and some problems were addressed. The team who was lecturing in the educational track was not completely satisfied with what the workshop had accomplished. As a result of the discussions a decision was made to create a preparatory course for the future educational workshop participants. The main problems addressed in that project were:

- The recruitment process had to be improved in order to select participants with sufficient English language skills. The selected participants should also find the educational track relevant for their personal professional needs.
- The pre-course should help cover some of the basic theory of learning and of general course design in order to give participants time to learn and practice the technology of designing on-line courses during the workshop.
- The pre-course should help to give a somewhat equal level of relevant knowledge for the participants who would enter the workshop.
- The pre-course should give the participants the opportunity to experience online learning themselves.

3. Approach

The main goals of the online pre-course were for participants to learn the basics of the pedagogy of open and distance learning and to gain experience from being a learner in online training. Compared to the Bratislava workshop, we would expect that participants of future workshops would be able to reach further in knowledge and skills in how to create online training.

Our approach was to use the web-based environment called WebCT, which is mentioned in the previous section. It is flexible, inexpensive and easy to obtain and can therefore be used after the pre-course for future course design in many different fields by the pre-course/workshop participants. WebCT has supporting functionality for contents, communication and collaboration, assessment and course administration. Contents can be integrated with functionality for interaction like self tests, glossary and of course hyperlinks to the Internet. Communication and collaboration is supported by a conferencing area with graphical representations of threaded discussions in multiple forums. It is also supported by a chat tool and by a presentation tool for groups of students to display their work in browsable html-format.

Part of our strategy was to make use of as much as was possible and suitable of the WebCT functionality in the pre-course. We wanted the participants to gain experiences from and insights into some of the strengths and weaknesses of online web-based techniques.

The online course was designed by more or less the same international team of lecturers that had met in Bratislava for the first educational track workshop. We were from Finland, Estonia and Sweden and apart from two face-to-face meetings we worked online designing the course, adding course material, developing assignments and assessment, and forming study groups.

4. Experiences and preliminary conclusions

Some preliminary conclusions drawn from the pre-course and workshop experience can be summed up as follows:

1. The pre-course had a strong positive impact on the selection of participants for the workshop. Some did not follow the course because it was not relevant to their present or future position, some because their workload was already too big, and some due to selection mechanisms unknown to us. In fact the selection was easily made from those people who actually finished the whole course, that is completed all the course assignments or, if not finished all assignments, yet took an active part in the course work and in the discussions. We ended up with 28 participants for the workshop, which was two less than the stipulated maximum number of 30 participants.
2. The participants were already prepared with a common frame of reference as to basic theoretical knowledge about course design in training, when arriving at the workshop.

This was a significant difference from the year before when most of the theoretical material was delivered in lectures during the workshop and it paved the way for the project-oriented activity during the workshop.

3. In the workshop the participants could draw heavily on their experiences from being on-line course participants in the pre-course. This experience had given them a shared knowledge of possibilities and drawbacks in learning online especially in the web-based course environment used. Quite a few of the participants' projects presented at the workshop stressed the importance of communication and collaboration. The opportunity to "meet" and discuss with people from different countries was one of the big issues of the WirEd course according to the participants. They also stressed the importance of the support from the teachers involved. We did not always meet the needs of the participants in this respect. On the other hand we opened "the floor" to the participants themselves to act and react to each other's solutions and opinions. The assignments were designed for collaboration and thus required a lot of communication in the process. It is obvious that the level and degree of interactivity among learners is important for their own learning. The participants' involvement in the interaction online also has to do with the sense on the part of the student of being the "owner" of the communication forum. If students perceive the discussion forum as being a teacher's resource they may hesitate to contribute (Phukan 1999).
4. The points 1 to 3 above show that in the special setting, as in this case, the web-based distance course was successful with respect to its main purposes. It would have been impossible to use a traditional course design with face-to-face sessions. The online option offered the participants the possibility to fit in the course work around their busy working schedules. It also gave the best solution with regard to the possibility of accessing the course regardless of time and place. The asynchronous mode for communication was especially well suited for our target group, since the span between the time zones was up to six hours for some participants.
5. During the creation and development of the pre-course the question of media choice for the team's collaboration was obvious. The online course environment opens up new possibilities for teachers in different places to co-operate. It offers an excellent arena for co-operation among teachers as well as for the participants. But it is not the answer to everything and since we had the possibility to choose media to a certain extent we used face-to-face meetings when we created the framework and outlined the contents of the pre-course. Other media could not easily have replaced these sessions with their social benefits of hard work and leisure! We also used telephone

conferencing during the assessment procedure, but the rest of the work was carried out online, using an e-mail distribution list and the WebCT environment.

When trying to comprehend new conceptions, it sometimes helps taking them to the extreme. In that respect our experience from the workshop and pre-course has helped us to some more understanding of educational media.

5. What next?

The communication technologies provide us educators with an enormous potential for delivering information to our students and for communicating with them. The real challenge is to balance content and process (Moore 1998), and to apply the learner-centred perspective to our pre-courses online.

Let's look at the next distance pre-course on the subject of online learning, WirEd II, as an opportunity to gain more knowledge about networked learning and about the communication and collaboration processes involved.

Our view on collaborative constructivist conceptions of learning is based on cultural-historical (or socio-cultural) grounds, which very briefly means that learning has to do with how people internalise and master tools for thinking and acting, and that teaching has to do with how to support that kind of constructivist learning. Communication is viewed as inseparable from the learning process. (Bakhtin 1996, Wertsch 1998, Vygotsky 1934/87). We believe that the interaction in the study groups is crucial for successful learning in distance courses.

Our view of the distance learner - who stays on - is that of a highly motivated and focused person who may not have the best environmental conditions for studying. So what all distance learners want and deserve is:

1. content and materials that they feel are relevant, interesting and useful
2. clear directions for what they should do at every stage of the course
3. control of the pace of the course
4. support on a personal basis in some way
5. feedback on results and progress

(Adapted from Moore 1998, p 4).

These are features that have been developed and used in distance learning for many years. In later years the importance of the communication and support between learners has been recognized (Turkel 1995). "These communities are different from their face-to-face and place-bound communities, but we cannot deny that they are meeting diverse social and intellectual need of widely distributed individuals." (Anderson & Garrison 1998 p. 103). Especially the computer mediated communication has the potential of supporting collaborative work (Harasim et al 1995). Interviews with WirEd participants have shown the importance of discussions and support from study group members, to keep going in spite of severe problems with slow connections.

The individual online learner's needs of support in terms of feedback, clear directions and personal support as indicated in the list above, can to some extent be met by the interaction between students. This, we believe, has a potential to contribute to the success of online training and education. As teachers and course designers we should try to learn more about participants' interaction and try to realise what the mechanisms are that support this kind of communication and collaboration online and how we can activate these mechanisms. We will point out a few ways that may be worth considering.

1. Design a variety of assignments that require both individual and group work
2. Stress the responsibility of the study group, define what constitutes fruitful collaboration online and include it in the evaluation.
3. Recognise the strengths of asynchronous communication in itself and learn more about the conditions for successful interaction online.

The assignments should aim at authenticity and relevance (Bruce & Rubin 1993) for the learner but also to varying degrees involve other course participants. When the assignment is an individual one (in the pre-course for example presenting an outline for an online course of one's own) the other participants are requested to give response, not only the teachers. The response can be both spontaneous and structured, for example checklists or questions, in order to help the learners focus on important issues.

Attention should be paid to learner attitudes and expectations in the online interaction. Would the following quotation from a posting be identified as a kind of stopper: "Maybe it's the time to begin 'hard' work. What do you think, our teachers? I hope the next week will be more useful and interesting." (WirEd 1999, article 83) This may reflect a laid-back attitude where the teacher is expected to have the responsibility for the activities of the study group and tell the participants how to solve the group assignment, which was described in the course material. Teachers are normally quite used to telling the student how to solve problems so it may be a new stance to take to put the responsibility where it should be, with the active participant! In WirEd one of the learning goals was to experience and cope with problems of collaboration online.

Other contributions reflected a much more active attitude, like this posting with comments intertwined with quotations from the previous letter:

Dear Zzzzzz!
I can design our logo, but first
>off all we must agree what is our group name.

Dear Xxxxx!
Glad to hear you from you again!

As I said in one of my previous messages, I don't know if it isn't to soon to make any decisions, as there are only three of us, and we don't know what the rest think.
>I am familiar
>with html too. I suggest to present photo in web page.

Great suggestion! I must admit I have a very poor memory for names: - Well, I think it's time we started working without waiting for the rest of our group. What do you think? And Yyyyy, what's your opinion?

Looking forward to hearing from you both, Zzzzzz

These participants took on the responsibility for the first assignment and started negotiating the tasks and plan their work, so that everybody would have a say. "Responsibility is a key issue in a collaborative constructivist perspective of teaching and learning" (Anderson & Garrison 1998, p 100). It might be rewarding to study what messages triggered reactions or actions and in what situations intentions failed. "The control model" (Andersson & Garrison 1998, p. 99) captures the importance of balance between three components that are essential to meaningful learning: independence, support and proficiency. Independence means that the learner is free to choose and follow his or her learning goals, yet avoiding the risk for isolation. Support has to do with both human support, from other participants and the tutor, and non-human support, for example from course material of all sorts. Proficiency describes the ability to learn, to construct meaning, and to keep on doing so throughout the course. To get a full picture of the learning situation the "interpretive" evaluation should be carried out together with the participants. The situation in this case should also be defined as the whole learning context which includes the working environment regarding Internet access and other equipment, time allowed for studying at work etc.

We should avoid comparing the interaction online with the interaction face-to-face in a way that simply stresses the shortcomings of text-based communication. "The capacity to support interaction in an asynchronous format provides an opportunity for reflection and deliberation not found in any synchronous learning environment - including the face-to-face classroom." (Anderson & Garrison 1998, p 103).

What we are saying is that we intend to learn from the future CEENet pre-courses how to activate and support collaboration among participants in their study groups and also evaluate how participants may help each other in the learning process, stressing the responsibility issue. We also intend to evaluate the use of the asynchronous mode of communication. In doing so we will take into account the differences between participants in time used for study work, the differences in bandwidth and access to the Internet, the possibility to re-organise regular work which has to be carried out over the same period etc. In studying the strengths and weaknesses of the asynchronous communication per se we will avoid using face-to-face communication as the frame of reference. In all this we must not forget to balance content and process; neither must be neglected in the continuing development of the pre-courses of the CEENet tracks.

References

[1] Andersson, T. D. & Garrison, D. R. (1998). Learning in a Networked World. In: *Distance Learners in Higher Education. Institutional Responses for Quality Outcomes.* Ed. C. C. Gibson. Atwood Publishing.

[2] Bakhtin, M. (1996). *Speech Genres & Other Late Essays.* Austin: University of Texas Press. (First published 1986. Sixth paperback printing, 1996).

[3] Berge, Z. (1995). Facilitating computer conferencing. Recommendations from the field. *Educational technology*, 35(1), 22-30.

[4] Bruce, B. & Rubin, A. (1993). *Electronic Quills. A Situated Evaluation of Using Computers for Writing in Classrooms.*
Hillsdale, NJ: Lawrence Erlbaum Associates, Publishers.

[5] Harasim, L. et al (1995). *Learning Networks. A Field Guide to Teaching and Learning Online.* The MIT Press. Third edition.

[6] Moore, M. G (1998). Introduction to Distance Learners in Higher Education. *Institutional Responses for Quality Outcomes.*
Ed. C. C. Gibson. Atwood Publishing.

[7] Phukan, Sanjeev (1999). "Delivering Courses Via The Web: Rethinking And Redesigning After First Experiences."
ENABLE99: Enabling Network-Based Learning.

URL: http://www.enable.evitech.fi/enable99/papers/phukan/phukan.html - Accessed: June 1999.

[8] Turkel, S. (1995). *Life on the Screen. Identity in the Age of the Internet.* New York: Simon & Shuster.

[9] Vygotsky, L. S. (1934/1987). Thinking and Speech. In Rieber, R. W. & Carton, A. S. (Eds). *The Collected Works of L. S. Vygotsky.* Volume 1: Problems of General Psychology. New York: Plenum Press.

[10] Wertsch, J. V. (1998). *Mind as Action.* New York: Oxford University Press.

Network Empowerment
O.B. Popov (Ed.)
IOS Press, 2004

Gajane Valcheuskaya

Comparative Analysis of Web-based e-learning Environments

The goal of the paper is to propose principles for comparison and assessment of virtual learning environments (VLEs), as well as to evaluate some of the most popular integrated e-learning environments.

Expert knowledge in comparisons and assessments are used to guide educators who care about expanding the implementation of information technology to improve educational service on different levels - institution, national and regional, as well - to make the most effective and substantiated choice and use of the available set of VLEs.

There are *different approaches* for comparing of VLEs. We distinguish between the pedagogical approach and the functionalities/feature approach. To combine both approaches while investigating software tools for e-courses delivery is a comprehensive task. However its solution allows to look beyond *table of functions* to understand not only *what the application does, "but how it does it, and whether it does it in a way which is appropriate to our needs"* [1].

Web-based software packages for electronic learning are divided as integrated, containing a broad range of teaching/learning capabilities and opportunities that allow to organize content into classroom-like formats, and specialized, emphasizing a particular aspect of e-course delivery. The principle advantage of integrated web-based software packages is combination of Internet access with several applications (e.g., e-mail, group discussion, multimedia, testing applications) "in one box" [3].

Examples of integrated packages are: WebCT, Blackboard, Learning Space, TopClass, FirstClass, and Virtual-U. These class management systems integrate into the common environment with the traditional features such as registration, group rosters, class scheduling, lectures, group and individual assignments, chat rooms, threaded discussions, student records, grading, and rich set of tools for administration of learning process.

Examples of specialized packages are: NetForum (University of Wisconsin) supporting group discussions; WebAssign (North Carolina State University (NCSU) providing automatic testing and grading facility; ToolBook Asymetrix/Instructor supporting creation of e-curricular.

Model for VLEs comparison presented in [3] classifies software depending on complexity of platforms mastering, termed as CPM model. Considering superposition of model CPM with the concept of integrated and specialized VLEs, presented above, we come to a conclusion that integrated VLEs may be considered as "*Delivery*" or "*Containers*" and specialized VLEs divided roughly into **two** categories:

Developer – typically multimedia software for web-production with some tools for realization of administrative capabilities. S*erious programming or scripting* required for effective utilization of these systems that is a barrier for non IT specialists. Examples of such platforms are: AuthorWare, IconAuthor, ToolBook II Instructor.

Instructor – "developer-tools-made-simple". *No-programming-required systems* are "ideal for the subject matter expert", but they *lose in capacity and variety* in comparison to Developer tools. Example - ToolBook II Assistant.

Let us identify the individuals who are involved in delivering of e-course. They are the course developer (author - content expert) and/or designer, the system and course administrator, the instructor (tutor or teaching assistant - TA), and the student.

In our evaluation of virtual learning environments (VLEs), we have been looking at three of the commercial applications most widely used in US and Eastern and Central European countries higher Education, currently - WebCT (The University of British Columbia, Canada), Blackboard (Blackboard Inc., Washington D.C., US), Learning Space (IBM).

Initially, we have allocated the following key items for *functionalities comparison* to look *what the application does*:

- Course layout (Structure of the course)
- Course content creation. Course developer perspective
  - o Course Design
  - o Content distribution
- Communication
- Collaborative work (course study groups)
- Quizzing infrastructure: features, security, question types
- Evaluation and grading
- Course Management

- Course Navigation
- Course effectiveness evaluation: student performance monitoring
- General Properties
- Technical Requirements
- Cost and Support

Course layout (Structure of the course)

Feature	Learning Space	Blackboard	WebCT
Structure of a course	There are *5 major areas*/databases to a Learning Space course: 1. Schedule 2. Media Center 3. Course Room 4. Profiles 5. Assessment Manager **Schedule** usually acts as a skeleton of a course. It contains curriculum of the course, links to websites, and schedule of activities, linked to the resources in Media Center. From the **Schedule** you can click on any activity and begin an assignment or participate in the discussion in *Course Room*, or you can go to the *Media Center* and study the resources. **Media Center** is a course material repository. It contains different types of resources used in the course, such as lecture notes, audio and video files, interactive exercises, glossaries, self tests, etc. Documents are collected as a list sorted out by Title, Writer, Keyword, and Type. Besides, there are links to a	There are *9 major areas* in a Blackboard class: 1. Announcements 2. Course Information 3. Staff Information 4. Course Documents 5. Assignments 6. Communication 7. External Links 8. Student Tools 9. Control panel **Announcements** - the first page within a course; it displays announcements about appearance of tests and assignment, or everything TA considers necessary announcing. **Course Information** contains such items as a *syllabus*, or a *reading list* or/ and links to weekly agendas. **Staff Information** contains information about course creators and conductors - authors, tutors(s), course administrators; office hours, office location, telephone, etc. **Course Documents** contains lecture notes, readings, links to websites, etc. **Assignment** contains assignments for each week.	Because WebCT is *entirely configurable*, there is only *1 major area* – the *front page* of a course. WebCT is a single system that allows **Custom Course Layout**

Feature	Learning Space	Blackboard	WebCT
	Course Room is a virtual classroom, developed for collaboration by means of private or public discussion, collaborative group work; as well as for reading, preparing and sending assignments. **Profile** database contains info about students and instructors. There are both a mini-homepage for each student and personal portfolio with student's grades. **Assessment Manager** database allows quizzes and tests creation as well as tracking student records. Here TA grades tests and other assignments, and keeps a grade book for tracking participants progress. It is for instructor use only. Created assignments are placed into the *Schedule* for students, who sent completed assignments back to *the Assessment Manager* for grading. Graded assignments are posted to the students' *Portfolio* in the *Profile database.* The Schedule is the "road map" for a course similar to a syllabus [2]. It guides designer through tasks to be completed and the materials needed to this work.	**Communication** may be used for - e-mail exchange, - discussion board - virtual classroom - chat conversations - students pages (group-based homepages) - one can view info about classmates - student roster **External Links** is a specific place for author to publish links to external websites that take you outside BB course. **Student Tools** may be used for - editing course homepages - change students information – password or personal information (optional) - reading student manual (optional) – walks through features in Bb - area provides students with possibilities for turn in - assignments, check grades and student calendar. **Control panel -** where an author adds/ correct content, create quizzes and surveys, online gradebook, and controls the course. Control panel is visible only to and/or TA.	

Feature	Learning Space	Blackboard	WebCT
	Linking you directly to the content, The Schedule "presents the structure and details of your course, such as assignment resources, learning objectives, overviews, reading materials, exercises, surveys and tests. The Schedule may be organized for self-paced learning with no specified due dates, or it may map you to a particular time frame that uses dates for completion. Depending on the design of your assignments, you can directly start a discussion or assignment from a Schedule document" [2]. LS supports direct import of designer's material into the Media Center.		
	Support hierarchical outline model and templates also Most of these areas may be turned off if the author does not want to use them		Author defines appearance of the course choosing from large number of set of capabilities.
	The author is free to make a decision how to use the platforms – as a combination with in-person class (for example, simply to post grades from a traditional class; to organize discussions on a forum) or as the foundation of an on-line class.		

In contrast to the other "Delivery" tools, WebCT supposes total flexibility re **what course components will be included** and considerable flexibility re the **'look' of the site** (backgrounds, document formatting etc.) [4].
Template creation is provided so that courses could meet an organization identity/standard. Alternatively, WebCT assumes instruments to customize a course thus, to fit an author's style. In both cases sound navigational elements are retained.
The option to customize the layout of the course makes design process more intuitive and enjoyable and enables to create products that fit with ones particular needs and teaching methods.

Course layout customization: to make each course completely unique

Feature	Learning Space	Blackboard	WebCT
Custom course layout	No	No	Yes
	Customization Libraries supports possibility to replace the existing course graphics with own logos or artwork.Layout for course Welcome page may be chosen from a large set of page layouts.	• Headers, • footers, and • navigation menus cannot be changed. Colors can be customized for the buttons, the banner and the background only, limiting course designers **with freedom in constructing and customizing the student experience in their course**.	• Headers, • footers, • navigation menus, • and colors can be changed.
	No	No	Yes
		Does not allow icons to be added or removed	• Banners, • backgrounds and • images can be uploaded.

Course Design: course content creation and distribution.

Selection of a particular VLE has a strong impact upon a course designer as techniques for course material uploading and incorporating into the VLE differ for different systems. Typically, the content is prepared outside of e-learning platform and then imported. Content modification depends on how content is delivered in WebCT. Most teachers create content (web pages) off-line using a web editor or application capable of saving web pages (Word, Wordperfect). The files are uploaded and linked with the appropriate tool (Single Page, Content Module). Except for minor changes, most faculties will go back to the original file to make modifications and re-upload the files. Students can "compile" the pages in a content module for downloading and offline viewing. However, all connections are no longer available that link the "complied" content to other functions in WebCT.

Feature	Learning Space	Blackboard	WebCT
Adding course material via...	the *Lotus Notes client program*	the *Control Panel of the course*.	the *file manager/uploading tool*

The important question for designer is *what media to use?* The VLEs allow any media types to be used as part of the course content, including text and/ or HTML documents, audio and image file formats, animations, movie clips, interactive applets and streaming audio and video, supported by the browsers and its "plug-ins". The question - streaming versus download-and-play media – is resolved in dependence of technical parameters of local networks. In WebCT, for example, multimedia files may be stored on an institution's server or accessed from the student's local CD-ROM drive. Adding multimedia elements to courses increase student involvement in the course content, as well as the student performance.

Feature	Learning Space	Blackboard	WebCT
Mutimedia	is supported in many ways. Any type of multimedia can be used. Multimedia files from the web can easily be access via URL links. Additionally, imports spreadsheets from MS office.	accepts 36 different mime types	is supported in many ways. Any type of multimedia can be used. Multimedia files from the web can easily be access via URL links
Links to external web sites	Yes but not available with browser access in Forum	Yes	Yes
CD-ROM tool			WebCT does have a "CD-ROM" tool that will allow access to multimedia (images, audio, video) located on a local drive (usually CD-ROM) instead of server-resident files.
Archive support			WebCT supports searchable image archive

There are several key features which are available only as part of the WebCT e-learning environment, as illustrated below

<table>
<tr><th>Feature</th><th>Learning Space</th><th>Blackboard</th><th>WebCT</th></tr>
<tr><td rowspan="2">Selective Release</td><td colspan="2">No
There is no equivalent option in these platforms.</td><td rowspan="2">Yes</td></tr>
<tr><td>If need TA can offer help in the Course Room</td><td></td></tr>
<tr><td>Content Modules</td><td>No</td><td>No</td><td>Yes</td></tr>
</table>

Feature	Learning Space	Blackboard	WebCT
			In contrast to other platforms Content Modules allow to organize course content into *structured content sequences* since WebCT provides the ability to create *separate content modules.* Selectively releasing those modules based on specific events, TA can dynamically manage student's movement through course content, as they "deem appropriate to meet the learning objectives of the course". More in, Content Modules also add automatic navigation to the content pages. There is a choice of reading the pages either sequentially or at any order one's prefers, without extra work required on the course designer.
Glossary	No	No	Yes The option of incorporating a glossary is supported. The glossary tool gives easy access to course terminology and definitions, with the ability to link to other words in the glossary or to outside web sites.

Selective Release is a critical feature in an VLE because it allows TA to release specific course modules such as e-lectures, assignments, or exams to individual students or to groups of students on a base of **defined parameters** like dates (timed basis) and student performance (performance basis). This feature enable individualized approach to teaching and learning process.

Ease of Course Design

Feature	Learning Space	Blackboard	WebCT
WebCourse Builder for novice course designers to get started quickly	No	No	Yes Allows quickly put together first course
The Syllabus tool	No	No	Yes Helps new users easily create their syllabi, using pre-defined sections or adding custom sections.
The **Designer Map** - the control center for course design, helping to orient users to the options available to them.	No	No	Yes The **Designer Map** in an easy to digest format. It is a single screen with links to all of the Course Utilities, Course Components and Tools
Community for extreme teaching for "extreme" (advanced) designers	No	No	Yes
Building upon the course content and structure supplied by one of publishing partners	Yes	Yes	Yes

Communication and collaborative work tools

Collaborative learning - an important element of engineering the pedagogigal elements in the course. Analyzed VLEs provide many ways of communication - asynchronous and synchronous as well - which support discussion groups and on-line recitations thus, mimics the situation of face-to-face learning. With the help of synchronous tools participants can work in a real time.

<table>
<tr><th colspan="3">Feature</th><th>Learning Space</th><th>Blackboard</th><th>WebCT</th></tr>
<tr><td rowspan="3">Communication</td><td colspan="2">Communication Center</td><td>CourseRoom area</td><td>Communication area</td><td>Because WebCT is completely configurable, there is no central area for Communication.</td></tr>
<tr><td rowspan="2">Asynchronous</td><td>E-mail
In what modes e-mails can be sent?</td><td>Instructors and students can email each other by clicking on the email links in the Profiles area.
Notes-type e-mail dynamically translated into internet protocol.</td><td colspan="2">E-mail exchange can be organized between everyone connected with the course and can be sent to either an individual or several people all at once.</td></tr>
<tr><td>Internal Course E-mail</td><td>No</td><td>No</td><td>Yes
E-mails circulate and are stored in the frames of the platform</td></tr>
</table>

		Feature	Learning Space	Blackboard	WebCT
Communication		**Threaded discussions** (viewed with topics and related comment threaded together for convenient reviewing) **BBS file exchange**[1]	LS files are not exchanged thorough a BBS. Typically files are exchanged in Media Center or in the *Course Room* area provides the opportunity for threaded discussions.	*Discussion Board* with possibility to create *multiple discussion boards* is supported. DB must be set initially by instructor.	*Bulletin Board* with possibility to create *multiple bulletin boards* (called "*forums*") which might focus on – different parts of the course or – specific groups.
		Link discussion to a concrete chapter/ module of course material that are related to the discussion	The thread. discussions and work assignments can be linked to assignment in the Schedule and Media Center resources		
		Newsgroups	The *Course Room* is newsgroup option.	*Yes*	*Yes*
	Synchronous	**Chat** The function allows for real time communication between course participants.	Yes	*Yes* Online office hours. Conversations from chat sessions and Discussion Board sessions are recorded and archived as part of Bb archiving process.	Yes Each group has 6 chat rooms. Room 1-4 can be archived, which mimics the behavior of a bulletin board. Room 5 is not archived, and room 6 is both not archived and open to all participants.

[1] BBS file exchange is the facility for download files and upload/post them over the web.

Feature			Learning Space	Blackboard	WebCT
Communication	**Synchronous**	**Voice chat**	No	Yes with Horizon Live	*Yes*
		Whiteboard	No/Yes Available in Collaboration Module	Yes with Tutor Net	*Yes*
Course study groups			YesThe Course Room supports the set up of groups. Is a possibility to choose the privacy level for discussion.	Yes with group projects	*Yes*

Quizzing infrastructure: testing and drilling within e-learning platforms

Assessment tools include self-tests, surveys, and quizzes. All systems provide instruments that can be used to construct tests or quizzes. Distinguishes between two types of assessments - test and quizzes – quizzes may employ only multiple choice or essay questions, and tests may in addition have fill-in and matching questions.

<table>
<tr><th>Feature</th><th>Learning Space</th><th>Blackboard</th><th>WebCT</th></tr>
<tr><td></td><td></td><td></td><td>According to analysis [4] WebCT's assessment and evaluation facilities are more comprehensive than any of the other platforms.</td></tr>
<tr><td rowspan="3">Supported question formats</td><td colspan="3">1. _ True - false
2. _Multiple Choice_
Students select either one or multiple correct answers to a question
2.1. _Multiple answer questions can be created by setting more than one answer in a multiple choice question as correct
2.2. True and false questions can be simulated by using a multiple choice question with two choices (one true, the other, false).
3. _Paragraph (essay, free form)_
Students answer in a longer essay-type format. The designer or the TA must grade this type of question manually.</td></tr>
<tr><td></td><td colspan="2">4. _Matching_
Students match items in two columns
5. _Short Answer
Students enter a word or short phrase, which is then matched against the possible answers.</td></tr>
<tr><td></td><td>6. _Ordering_</td><td>6. _Calculated_
Students answer a mathematical question. Mathematical formula and the set of variables, along with a range of values for each variable. A set of answers is generated for a randomly selected set of variables.</td></tr>
</table>

Feature	Learning Space	Blackboard	WebCT
Question pool	One can create a question pool, but an entire question pool can not be imported from a format outside…		
	of Learning Space. Question databank locates in the Assessment Manager database. Here questions can be inputted and stored.	of Blackboard CourseInfo.	of WebCT environment.
Timed quizzes	Yes	Yes	Yes

Quizzing infrastructure: What quiz security tools are provided by investigated VLEs?

Advanced Quizzing Security features includes question randomization, IP masks, proctor passwords, calculation variables and individual question serving. All these features WebCT is provided in contrast to other systems [4].

Feature	Learning Space	Blackboard	WebCT
Randomized questions	Yes	Yes	Yes
Questions with randomly generated parameters (e.g., sin ax + sin by = c, where a, b, and c are randomly generated)	Yes	Yes	Yes
In multiple choice questions randomization of order of correct answers	Yes	Yes	Yes
IP masks	No	No	Yes
Proctor password	No	No	Yes
Calculation variables	No	No	Yes
Individual question serving	Yes	Yes	Yes
Advanced Quizzing Security	No	No Does not provide a comprehensive set of security features [4].	Yes

Evaluation and grading: records and logging student performance assessments

The VLEs provide tools for maintaining an on-line grade book and for making grade reports accessible and for students and instructors.

<table>
<tr><th>Feature</th><th>Learning Space</th><th>Blackboard</th><th>WebCT</th></tr>
<tr><td rowspan="2">Auto grading</td><td colspan="3">YesAll question types except for essay/paragraph (which must be scored manually) are auto-graded and reported to the on-line grade book. Students may access the grade book to review their individual grades.</td></tr>
<tr><td>The entire test may be set to be auto-graded. However, the instructor must begin the grading process either by choosing to grade all the tests in the queue if auto-grading has been selected for the test or specifically grading each test.</td><td colspan="2">If the test consists entirely of auto-graded questions, than the entire test will be auto-graded when it is turned in.</td></tr>
<tr><td>Automatic grade logging from on-line quiz forms</td><td>Yes</td><td>Yes</td><td>Yes</td></tr>
<tr><td>Built-in grade book</td><td>Yes</td><td>Yes</td><td>Yes</td></tr>
<tr><td rowspan="3">Use of the grade book</td><td colspan="3">Graded tests are kept in the graded assessment database.</td></tr>
<tr><td>Any assignment which has been created within the Lotus Notes can be assigned a grade. All graded items appear in the Assessment database.</td><td colspan="2">Any assignment, whether it was created in BB, WebCT or not, can be entered in the grade book.</td></tr>
<tr><td>Information from the Assessment database can be exported to a text file</td><td colspan="2">The grade book can be exported to a text file which is easily imported into an Excel spreadsheet.</td></tr>
</table>

Feature	Learning Space	Blackboard	WebCT
Grade book: availability of grades for students	or a Lotus 1-2-3 worksheet and from there put into an Excel spreadsheet, but this is not a neat, easy process.	Blackboard even gives you step by step instructions on the procedure	
Report of class statistics for quizzes visiable to student and TA			If appropriate settings are chosen by instructor, students may obtain **class performance measurements** including the test mean, median, maximum, and minimum scores.

Ease of Course Management

In response to faculty desire minimize time spent for course management WebCT has developed tools, unavailable in other platforms. While main competitors does offer management features such as a "basic way to compile student grades [4], WebCT moves decisively beyond these basics" and provides instructors with …

Feature	Learning Space	Blackboard	WebCT
The ability to seamlessly track student performance and online participation	Yes, but not so flexible and versatile as in WebCT		Yes
	Instructor can track indiv. or group progress in the Course Room in discussions or assignments and tests.		
Advanced File Management	No	No Basic ability to upload and download files. In the Bb system designer has very little organization and tracking capabilities over files **unless the designer is at the specific computer that contains the course files (server)**.	Yes. It allows to upload and download regular as well as zipped files, copy, rename and delete files. Designer can manage, organize and edit course content "behind the scenes", using different directories, which are linked to the course. WebCT File Manager supports more advanced file management and more convenience The WebCT File Manager allows design a course **from any computer connected to the Internet**.
Internal Course Email (important course management and communication tool)	No	No	Yes Allows course participants _to access, _track, _document, and _respond to course specific email in central location. Thus, instructors have a simple, archived system of communication.

Method of Access

Every user of web-based software platform plays one of the following roles presented in the table below. Different roles determine different access to the material of the course: no access, read only, read and write, full access. User ID set up the degree of access (from read only to full). The administrator determines who is able to access each module/chunk of course material.

Feature	Learning Space	Blackboard	WebCT
Levels of access	**4 levels of access** • student, • instructor, • facilitator, • or administrator. The availability of anonymous access (no password) or a restriction to password protected access is determined separately in each course.	**4 levels of access** • student, • instructor, • facilitator, or administrator.	**5 levels of access** • students • instructor (author) • TA • guest • administrator The availability of anonymous access (no password) or a restriction to password protected access is determined separately in each course.
	The software, built *on Lotus Notes databases*. It can be accessed by learner either from *Lotus Notes client* or from a web browser, like Netscape.	The only thing one needs to either **administer** or **design or take** a *Blackboard/ WebCT* class is an Internet connection (access to the web) and web browsers such as Netscape or MS Explorer.	
Method of access	—— This is the same for **student** or **Instructor** access in *Learning Space*. **Instructor** can get into the course via the web to view what students see or participate in a conversation in the Course Room. In web browser an address of the server, containing the course should be typed in the Location bar, say http://www.policy.hu. Later this address can be bookmarker and accessed from the menu of a browser.		
	In order to **administer** a course in Learning Space, the instructor must have the **Lotus Notes client program** loaded on their computer. **Author cannot change/update course materials via the Web interface.**		

Ease of Course Navigation

Important elements are both an intuitive user interface and easy and flexible system of course navigation.

Feature	Learning Space	Blackboard	WebCT
Highly Customizable Course Menu	No Icons at the bottom of the page allow you to go to the previous/next/top pages, or to open help window or to access an already created a bookmark	No Bb has buttons for navigation, but the	Yes WebCT course menu allows *to quickly move forward and backward* to any course part and to have all major important parts of the course accessible from a single location. Course menu can be customized to a significant percent by designer.
	WebCT course menu is much more flexible convenient		
Breadcrumbs	No	No	Yes While moving through the course, the *"Breadcrumbs"* signal as to where you are, and where you have been as well, inside of a course.
Resume	No	No	Yes There is the option to *Resume* a lesson when you re-enter a course and to *Auto-Forward.* "These navigation options, among others, increase the user's efficiency, allowing the focus to be on the teaching and learning process rather than the technology" [4].
Auto-Forward	No	No	Yes An interactive chart that correlates teaching tasks and WebCT tools. "This pedagogical reference guide is extremely helpful to instructors teaching online for the first time" [4]
Designer Map	No	No	Yes

Course effectiveness evaluation: student performance monitoring

Feature	Learning Space	Blackboard	WebCT
Student tracking features. (Possibility to TA/student to track, monitor, and log student access to content pages)	Student may keep a "My work progress folder" for monitoring assignments and overall progress during the course		Yes *Instructors* can monitor how a student moves through the course and can also evaluate their course structure by analyzing their page tracking data. Direct information can be obtained in an anonymous fashion through surveys and anonymous discussion topics. "Page reference statistics/ reference patterns may indicate the degree to which a given student is participating in the course" [4].

Technical requirements

Feature	Learning Space	Blackboard	WebCT
Platforms	Lotus Notes/Domino server	UNIX and windows NT	UNIX and windows NT

Conclusions

On the surface, it appears that there are no great differences between the examined and compared platforms. However, the experienced users of these VLEs know that **there are indeed many differences as soon as you go deep into the platform and use it.**[5-8]. The actual choice of a platform to is always a matter of compromise.

We have chosen WebCT course management system because it provides a full range of tools for various teaching methodologies. Currently, the platform offers the richest and the most flexible suite of pedagogically sound tools [4].

A *major drawback* might be the requirement for the designer to spent a lot of time on-line in order to modify the content of the course. On the other hand, the list of Web CT platform advantages is impressive is:

- Does not require technical expertise
- It is intuitive and easy-to-use with a minimal training
- Flexible in instructional design
  - easy to build and modify
  - supporting multiple author course design from remote locations
  - providing co-teaching ability for multiple instructors
  - enables custom course layout; the designer is able to construct a unique course from full range of modules
  - supporting variety of multimedia formats
- The user interface is easy to understand, as well as the navigation
- An open architecture that supports third-party learning applications, interfaces, and system services to seamlessly interact with the" WebCT platform [9]
- It can run on the both UNIX and Windows servers
- It used to be inexpensive to licence (which is not true any more)
- Offeres course and content authoring tools, synchronous and asynchronous collaboration tools, a robust assessment engine, and excellent features that enable students to track, monitor and assess their progress

References

[1] WebCT vs Blackboard http://www.ltss.bris.ac.uk/interact21/in21p04.htm.
S. Bayne, J. Cook, Learning Technology Support Service, UK; 4.

[2] Learning Space Guide http://www.worldbank.org/distancelearning

[3] EdTec 650 Technology Demonstration http://edweb.sdsu.edu/Courses/ET650_Online/Fall_97/LRSmith650/index.html#Comparisons

[4] Key differences between WebCT and Blackboard. WebCT. WebCT, November 2000, http://www.webct.com.

[5] Why WebCT? http://www.sheridanc.on.ca/academic/edserv/WCTwhy.htm, D. Galambos, Sheridan College.

[6] On-line educational delivery application: a web-tool for comparative analysis http://www.ctt.bc.ca/landonline/choices.html, http://www.c2t2.ca/landonline/evalapps.asp. Team of B. Landon, Douglas College.

[7] Comparison of web based course environments: http://www.edutech.ch/edutech/tools/grid_e.asp. Federal Office of Education and Science, the Swiss University Conference, the University of Fribourg.

[8] Relative Merits of Courseware Management Tools. http://www.succeed.vt.edu/info/RelativeMerits.htm

[9] http://www.balckboard.com

Authors

David Billard received his Ph.D. in Computer Science at the University of Montpellier (France) in 1995. From 1995 to 2000, he was a research fellow in the Computer Science Department of the University of Geneva, working on transactional systems on the Internet. Currently, he is head of the Application Development Services in the Computer Centre at the University of Geneva. He is also a lecturer in Computer Science at the University of Geneva and CEENet/NATO workshops, and serves as an expert in computer science to the legal authorities and the courts in France. Dr. Billard research interests include the Internet, Law on the Internet, Advanced Information Systems and Distributed Operating Systems.

Rolf Dalin is a lecturer in Statistics in the Institute for Information technology and Media at Mid Sweden University. Mr. Dalin holds a M.Sc. degree in Statistics from Uppsala University. In the last couple of years, Mr. Dalin has developed and used information technology in teaching and learning, as well as Web-supported methods for DE/Flexible Learning. In 1996, he was appointed a member of "The Society of Living Pedagogues", as one of the activities within the framework of the "Council for The Renewal of Undergraduate Education" in Sweden.

Karin Ekberg has a M.Sc. degree in Literature and Scandinavian languages from the Uppsala University, Sweden. Since the early nineties, she is a lecturer in communication and technical writing in the Institute of Information Technology and Media at Mid Sweden University. Mrs. Ekberg has a distinguished career in adult education, life-long learning, and course evaluation. As the Director of Studies, she has been responsible for in-service training and participatory learning. Mrs. Ekberg has designed and participated in numerous workshops and seminars on the pedagogical aspects of on-line courses, communication and collaborative work.

Francois Fluckiger is the Head of Internet Infrastructure at CERN, the European Particle Physics Laboratory and the birthplace of the World-Wide Web. He is also an adjunct professor of Computer Science at the University of Geneva. A member of the Internet Society Advisory Council and an author of the seminal book "Understanding Networked Multimedia", a Prentice Hall publication. Dr. Fluckiger has more than 28 years of experience in design and management of large-scale networks, including 18 years in the Internet technologies. He has graduated from the Ecole Supérieure d'Electricité and the Enterprise Administration Institute in Paris.

Ole J. Jacobsen has been active in the computer networking field since 1976, when he went to work for the Norwegian Defense Research Establishment, an early ARPANET site. Mr. Jacobsen was with Interop Company (now Ziff Davis) since shortly after its formation in 1987 until 1998. He was the Editor and Publisher of ConneXions - The Interoperability Report, a monthly technical journal in the field of computer communications, published by Interop Company.

Jacobsen has been a member of the Internet Society Advisory Council since 1994, and he served as Vice President for Chapters from 1998 to 1999. He serves on several programme committees for international networking events such as INET, APRICOT and NetWorld+Interop, and is a member of the Board of Directors of the Asia Pacific Internet Association (APIA).

Jacobsen holds a B.Sc. in Electrical Engineering and Computing Science from the University of Newcastle upon Tyne, England. He is the Editor and Publisher of The Internet Protocol Journal, a quarterly technical publication for Internet and intranet professionals published by Cisco Systems. In his spare time, Mr. Jacobsen enjoys playing and listening to pipe organs. He is a member of the American Guild of Organists, ACM and the House Rabbit Society.

David Martland is currently a lecturer in Computer Science at Kingston University, UK. Formerly, he was associated with Brunell University and thought Computer Science at Mid Sweden University from 1997 until 2001. Dr. Martland research interests include multimedia, caching and Web technologies, multicasting and using the Internet in the education.

Oliver B. Popov is a professor of Computer Science, at the Institute of Informatics, Faculty of Natural Sciences and Mathematics, Saints Cyril and Methodius University in Skopje, Macedonia, and was the President of the Executive Board of Macedonian Academic and Research Network (MARNet) from 1995 until 2002, where he is now a member. He holds a Ph.D. in Computer Science from the University of Missouri, USA. His research inclinations converge towards computer networks, distributed computing, protocol engineering and formal theories of knowledge. He is the Programme Director of the CEENet Network Technology Workshops since their inception in 1995, member of the CEENet Management Committee from 1995, Vice-chairman from 1999 to 2003 and Chairman of CEENet from 2003. From 2000 until 2002, Professor Popov served on the NATO Science Committee Computer Networking Panel. Since the fall of 2000, Dr. Popov is a professor of Computer Science in the Institute for Information Technology and Media at Mid Sweden University in Sweden.

Iskra Djonova-Popova is an assistant professor in the Faculty for Pedagogy at Saints Cyril and Methodius University in Skopje, Macedonia. She holds a Ph.D. in Computer Science from the Saints Cyril and Methodius University. The focus of her research is in routing protocols and algorithms for flow control, as well as the use of networks and the Internet technology in education. Currently, Dr. Popova is an associate professor in the Institute for Information Technology and Media at Mid Sweden University in Sweden.

Wolfgang Schneider studied at the Technical University Darmstadt. After working in the field of computer networking and computer communication for many years, he got fascinated by the problems of IT security and the opportunities of cryptography in the mid-eighties. Mr. Schneider participated in allegedly what was to become the first e-Commerce project in Europe 1985-86 (which included the use of RSA). The project eventually led to the foundation of Teletrust Germany where Mr. Schneider contributed from the very beginning. He is now head of the department "Security and Smartcard Technology" at GMD, and is also a project director of the European projects ICE-TEL (Public Key Infrastructure for the European R&D) and ICE-CAR (PKIs for Commerce, Administration and Research). Moreover, Mr. Schneider initiated and coordinated the Mailtrust development at Teletrust - Germany and is co-founder of SECUDE GmbH, a leading supplier of PKI and information security technology.

Gayane Valecheuskaja works for the Belarus Academy of Sciences where she is one of the key persons in the area of Information and Communication Technologies. Dr. Valecheuskaja has been a champion in the proliferation of Distance Learning in Belarus. In the course of her work in e-learning, she has had an extensive co-operation with CEENet, especially on the Tver Workshop and RuWirEd project.